Precepts & Principles
from Proverbs

Timeless Wisdom for Today

> He is educated who knows how to find out what he
> doesn't know. (Georg Simmel)

Other books by Rev. Amos L. Lewis:

Pearls of Wisdom for Everyday Living

Pearls of Wisdom Study Guide and Devotional

Pearls of Wisdom for Everyday Living Journal

The Blessing Book Daily Devotional

Precepts & Principles from Proverbs

Timeless Wisdom for Today

Rev. Amos L. Lewis

The Master of Simplicity

An Amethyst Moon book

AMETHYST MOON
PUBLISHING

Precepts & Principles from Proverbs
Timeless Wisdom for Today

Copyright ©2009 by Rev. Amos L. Lewis

Cover Photograph ©2009 by Diana Acosta

Unless otherwise indicated, all Scripture quotations are taken from the New Living Transation of the Bible.

An Amethyst Moon Book
Published by AMETHYST MOON PUBLISHING
P.O. Box 87885
Tucson, AZ 85754
www.onechoicecanchangealife.com

ISBN 978-1-935354-06-2 (13 digit)
1-935354-06-X (10 digit)

DEDICATION

This book is dedicated to my two grandsons, Jayden L. Lewis and Emmanuel Z. Holmes. It's my desire that they will learn the wisdom of God at an early age and grow up to be giants for God.

It is also dedicated to the young people at Rising Star. I see a fresh anointing on them. They are real and on fire for the Lord. I believe they will take the world by storm.

Lastly, this book is dedicated to all the young and old alike who would like to pursue, proclaim and publish the wisdom of God.

Educate children without religion and
you make a race of clever devils out of them.
(Arthor Wellesley, 1st Duke of Wellington)

Education is the most powerful weapon which you can
use to change the world. (Nelson Mandela)

What sculpture is to a block of marble, education is to a human soul. (Joseph Addison, 1672-1719, English Essayist, Poet, Statesman)

The greatest homage we can pay to truth is to use it. (James Russell Lowell, 1819-1891, American Diplomat, Poet, Critic, Editor)

ACKNOWLEDGMENTS

I want to thank all of those who supported me in making this book a reality. It's my goal to place a copy of this book in the hands of every young person out there. I want to thank my wife, Zeannie Lewis, for her continuous sacrifice and support. I wish to thank my children, Kevin, Jenelle, Jeremiah, and Terra, for allowing me to practice my wisdom on them down through the years. Many thanks to Tammie Brown for proofreading and editing the manuscript. Her ideas and help were invaluable. Cynthia Carr-Person, thank you for allowing me to bounce ideas off you and for your feedback.

I am grateful to the A. L. Lewis Ministries team for their behind the scene support in keeping the ministry up and running strong. Thank you to Min. Diana Acosta for her patience in taking pictures for the cover. Tandala Kidd, I truly appreciate you overseeing the business and keeping things on track. I want to thank all the members of Rising Star for their love and continued support as well as all the different organizations in the community for their support and vote of confidence.

I also want to thank my sisters, Vivian Thompson-Lewis, Annie Doris Howard, and my brother, Joe Lewis, for being my biggest cheerleaders.

Lastly, I thank God for my publisher, Lin Conklin, for her flexibility, support, strong work ethic, and encouragement.

CONTENTS

INTRODUCTION

While lying awake in bed one night, the Lord spoke to my heart and said, "Take the book of Proverbs and its 31 chapters and develop a devotional book." He also instructed me to use the "Pearls of Wisdom for Everyday Living" from my first book and include all the pearls from the book of Proverbs in this book. You will find these pearls in the boxes that look like the one to the right (the "X" is the number of the pearl as listed in *Pearls of Wisdom for Everyday Living*).

> **Pearls of Wisdom**
>
> X. These boxes contain pearls from the book of Proverbs as found in my first book, *Pearls of Wisdom for Everyday Living*.

I encourage you to keep this edition handy and write down your own notes and thoughts as you read. One of the things I said in my first book is, "An unread book can't help you." So it is with this book. It can only help you as you read it and heed it. You must meditate on the "precepts and principles" and then put them into practice.

You might ask the question, "What are principles and why do I need them?" Well, principles are universal and unchanging laws that will help you understand how the world works so you can safely and successfully navigate your way though the challenges of life.

You might be asking another question, "Who is the guy who wrote the Book of Proverbs?" Well his name is Solomon, the son of King David in the Old Testament. Solomon is considered by God to be both the wealthiest and wisest man to ever live. Solomon reminds us that wisdom is "a principle thing" (Prov. 4:7). Wisdom is the master key to all the treasures of life. When God asked Solomon, as a young man, what he wanted, Solomon asked for wisdom and God gave it to him (2 Chron. 1:7-12). Solomon created and collected wise sayings from others (1 Kings 4:29-34; Eccl. 12:9-10). God will give you wisdom also if you ask Him and seek for it (James 1:5).

> A chapter of Proverbs a day will keep foolishness and stupidity away. (Rev. Amos L. Lewis)

Proverbs 1

Wisdom Warns about Being Enticed by Sinners

The Purpose of Proverbs

¹ *These are the proverbs of Solomon, David's son, king of Israel.*

² *The purpose of these proverbs is to teach people wisdom and discipline, and to help them understand wise sayings.* ³ *Through these proverbs, people will receive instruction in discipline, good conduct, and doing what is right, just, and fair.* ⁴ *These proverbs will make the simpleminded clever. They will give knowledge and purpose to young people.*

⁵ *Let those who are wise listen to these proverbs and become even wiser. And let those who understand receive guidance* ⁶ *by exploring the depth of meaning in these proverbs, parables, wise sayings, and riddles.*

⁷ *Fear of the LORD is the beginning of knowledge. Only fools despise wisdom and discipline.*

Pearls of Wisdom

151. Education is powerful. The more you know the farther you will go. The more you learn the more you will earn (Prov. 1:5).

449. A wise person will become a student of successful people and organizations (Prov. 1:5).

72. Respect for God is the first step in gaining wisdom (Prov. 1:7).

A Father's Exhortation: Acquire Wisdom

[8] *Listen, my child, to what your father teaches you. Don't neglect your mother's teaching.* [9] *What you learn from them will crown you with grace and clothe you with honor.*

[10] *My child, if sinners entice you, turn your back on them!* [11] *They may say, "Come and join us. Let's hide and kill someone! Let's ambush the innocent!*

Pearl of Wisdom

459. Since God gave you a brain, make sure you do your own thinking (Prov. 1:10–19).

[12] *Let's swallow them alive as the grave swallows its victims. Though they are in the prime of life, they will go down into the pit of death.* [13] *And the loot we'll get! We'll fill our houses with all kinds of things!* [14] *Come on, throw in your lot with us; we'll split our loot with you."*

[15] *Don't go along with them, my child! Stay far away from their paths.* [16] *They rush to commit crimes. They hurry to commit murder.* [17] *When a bird sees a trap being set, it stays away.* [18] *But not these people! They set an ambush for themselves; they booby–trap their own lives!* [19] *Such is the fate of all who are greedy for gain. It ends up robbing them of life.*

Wisdom Shouts in the Streets

[20] *Wisdom shouts in the streets. She cries out in the public square.* [21] *She calls out to the crowds along the main street, and to those in front of city hall.* [22] *"You simpletons!" she cries. "How long will you go on being simpleminded? How long will you mockers relish your mocking? How long will you fools fight the facts?* [23] *Come here and listen to me! I'll pour out the spirit of wisdom upon you and make you wise.*

²⁴ *"I called you so often, but you didn't come. I reached out to you, but you paid no attention.* ²⁵ *You ignored my advice and rejected the correction I offered.* ²⁶ *So I will laugh when you are in trouble! I will mock you when disaster overtakes you –* ²⁷ *when calamity overcomes you like a storm, when you are engulfed by trouble, and when anguish and distress overwhelm you.*

²⁸ *"I will not answer when they cry for help. Even though they anxiously search for me, they will not find me.* ²⁹ *For they hated knowledge and chose not to fear the LORD.* ³⁰ *They rejected my advice and paid no attention when I corrected them.* ³¹ *That is why they must eat the bitter fruit of living their own way. They must experience the full terror of the path they have chosen.* ³² *For they are simpletons who turn away from me – to death. They are fools, and their own complacency will destroy them.* ³³ *But all who listen to me will live in peace and safety, unafraid of harm."*

Prayer: Lord, please help me to develop wisdom by respecting you and your Word. I know this is the surest and safest way to success. Help me not to be influenced by the negative things and people around me. Help me to make good decisions so not to go astray. Please help me to be an example to others. Keep my thoughts clean and my mind focused on you. In Jesus' Name I pray, Amen.

The mediocre teacher tells. The good teacher explains.
The superior teacher demonstrates. The great teacher
inspires. (William Arthur Ward)

Proverbs 2
Wisdom Saves from Evil and Pays Benefits

The Benefits of Wisdom

[1] *My child, listen to me and treasure my instructions.* [2] *Tune your ears to wisdom, and concentrate on understanding.* [3] *Cry out for insight and understanding.* [4] *Search for them as you would for lost money or hidden treasure.* [5] *Then you will understand what it means to fear the LORD, and you will gain knowledge of God.* [6] *For the LORD grants wisdom! From his mouth come knowledge and understanding.* [7] *He grants a treasure of good sense to the godly. He is their shield, protecting those who walk with integrity.* [8] *He guards the paths of justice and protects those who are faithful to him.*

Pearls of Wisdom

656. Wisdom gives wings to knowledge like wind gives flight to a kite (Prov. 2:1–6).

657. Wisdom is the proper application of knowledge (Prov. 2:1–6).

---

[9] *Then you will understand what is right, just, and fair, and you will know how to find the right course of action every time.* [10] *For wisdom will enter your heart, and knowledge will fill you with joy.* [11] *Wise planning will watch over you. Understanding will keep you safe.*

[12] *Wisdom will save you from evil people, from those whose speech is corrupt.* [13] *These people turn from right ways to walk down dark and evil paths.* [14] *They rejoice in doing wrong, and they enjoy evil as it turns things upside down.* [15] *What they do is crooked, and their ways are wrong.*

16 Wisdom will save you from the immoral woman, from the flattery of the adulterous woman. 17 She has abandoned her husband and ignores the covenant she made before God. 18 Entering her house leads to death; it is the road to hell. 19 The man who visits her is doomed. He will never reach the paths of life.

20 Follow the steps of good men instead, and stay on the paths of the righteous. 21 For only the upright will live in the land, and those who have integrity will remain in it. 22 But the wicked will be removed from the land, and the treacherous will be destroyed.

Prayer: Lord, I believe your Word. I know that I need your wisdom that enables me to avoid evil and to do what is right. I ask for your strength, especially during the times of temptation so that I can resist evil. I know that obedience to your Word will pay great dividends in the end. In Jesus' Name I pray, Amen.

Proverbs 3
Wisdom Results in Right Relationships and Gives Life and Honor

Trusting in the LORD

1 My child, never forget the things I have taught you. Store my commands in your heart, 2 for they will give you a long and satisfying life. 3 Never let loyalty and kindness get away from you! Wear them like a necklace; write them deep within your heart. 4 Then you will find favor with both God and people, and you will gain a good reputation.

Pearls of Wisdom

45. Listen to your quiet inner voice. It's your conscience telling you which way to go (Prov. 3:5–6; Rom. 8:14).

486. Your life today is a reflection of the choices you made yesterday (Prov. 3:5–6).

607. Following God is more a matter of the heart than the head (Prov. 3:5–6; Rom. 8:14).

702. Find out which way God is going and go that way (Prov. 3:5–6; Rom. 8:14).

782. Every decision you make affects your character (Prov. 3:5–6).

1011. Don't just live your life, lead your life by making good choices (Prov. 3:5–6).

1100. If more people would get in the health line, we would have less people in the healing line (Prov. 3:7–8).

401. If you continue to sow, eventually your life will kick into overflow (Prov. 3:9–10).

940. Live by the 80/10/10 rule. Give God 10%. Save or invest 10%. Live on the other 80% (Prov. 3:9–10; Mal. 3:8–10).

5 *Trust in the LORD with all your heart; do not depend on your own understanding.* 6 *Seek his will in all you do, and he will direct your paths.*

7 *Don't be impressed with your own wisdom. Instead, fear the LORD and turn your back on evil.* 8 *Then you will gain renewed health and vitality.*

9 *Honor the LORD with your wealth and with the best part of everything your land produces.* 10 *Then he will fill your barns with grain, and your vats will overflow with the finest wine.*

11 *My child, don't ignore it when the LORD disciplines you, and don't be discouraged when he corrects you.* 12 *For the LORD corrects those he loves, just as a father corrects*

a child in whom he delights.

[13] Happy is the person who finds wisdom and gains understanding. [14] For the profit of wisdom is better than silver, and her wages are better than gold. [15] Wisdom is more precious than rubies; nothing you desire can compare with her. [16] She offers you life in her right hand, and riches and honor in her left. [17] She will guide you down delightful paths; all her ways are satisfying. [18] Wisdom is a tree of life to those who embrace her; happy are those who hold her tightly.

[19] By wisdom the LORD founded the earth; by understanding he established the heavens. [20] By his knowledge the deep fountains of the earth burst forth, and the clouds poured down rain.

[21] My child, don't lose sight of good planning and insight. Hang on to them, [22] for they fill you with life and bring you honor and respect. [23] They keep you safe on your way and keep your feet from stumbling. [24] You can lie down without fear and enjoy pleasant dreams. [25] You need not be afraid of disaster or the destruction that comes upon the wicked, [26] for the LORD is your security. He will keep your foot from being caught in a trap.

[27] Do not withhold good from those who deserve it when it's in your power to help them. [28] If you can help your neighbor now, don't say, "Come back tomorrow, and then I'll help you."

²⁹ *Do not plot against your neighbors, for they trust you.* ³⁰ *Don't make accusations against someone who hasn't wronged you.*

³¹ *Do not envy violent people; don't copy their ways.* ³² *Such wicked people are an abomination to the LORD, but he offers his friendship to the godly.*

³³ *The curse of the LORD is on the house of the wicked, but his blessing is on the home of the upright.*

³⁴ *The LORD mocks at mockers, but he shows favor to the humble.*

³⁵ *The wise inherit honor, but fools are put to shame!*

Prayer: Lord, help me to develop good relationships. I know that the friends I have are a reflection of me. I also know that I cannot be wise without your wisdom. Therefore, please help me to find wise people to hang around so I can be all that you want me to be. I cannot make and maintain good relationships without you. I acknowledge that my relationship to you is the most important relationship, followed by my parents and then others. Lord, help me to get closer to you. In Jesus' Name I pray, Amen.

By learning you will teach; by teaching you will learn.
(Latin Proverb)

What greater or better gift can we offer the republic than to teach and instruct our young? (Cicero)

Proverbs 4
Wisdom Results in Self–discipline

A Father's Wise Advice

[1] *My children, listen to me. Listen to your father's instruction. Pay attention and grow wise,* [2] *for I am giving you good guidance. Don't turn away from my teaching.* [3] *For I, too, was once my father's son, tenderly loved by my mother as an only child.*

[4] *My father told me, "Take my words to heart. Follow my instructions and you will live.* [5] *Learn to be wise, and develop good judgment. Don't forget or turn away from my words.* [6] *Don't turn your back on wisdom, for she will protect you. Love her, and she will guard you.* [7] *Getting wisdom is the most important thing you can do! And whatever else you do, get good judgment.* [8] *If you prize wisdom, she will exalt you. Embrace her and she will honor you.* [9] *She will place a lovely wreath on your head; she will present you with a beautiful crown."*

Pearls of Wisdom

2. One great line of wisdom can be enough to change your entire life (Prov. 4:7).

756. Become a principle–centered person (Prov. 4:7).

860. Principles are proven guidelines for human behavior (Prov. 4:7).

[10] *My child, listen to me and do as I say, and you will have a long, good life.* [11] *I will teach you wisdom's ways and lead you in straight paths.* [12] *If you live a life guided by wisdom, you won't limp or stumble as you run.* [13] *Carry out my instructions; don't forsake them. Guard them, for they will lead you to a fulfilled life.*

¹⁴ *Do not do as the wicked do or follow the path of evildoers.* ¹⁵ *Avoid their haunts. Turn away and go somewhere else,* ¹⁶ *for evil people cannot sleep until they have done their evil deed for the day. They cannot rest unless they have caused someone to stumble.* ¹⁷ *They eat wickedness and drink violence!*

Pearls of Wisdom

242. The key to making progress in life is to build a perfect day and repeat it (Prov. 4:18). Every day is a new beginning.

670. Success is achieved one day at a time (Prov. 4:18).

1088. Success is progressive. Build on the previous day's success (Prov. 4:18).

205. Your tongue is connected to your heart (Prov. 4:20–23).

---

¹⁸ *The way of the righteous is like the first gleam of dawn, which shines ever brighter until the full light of day.* ¹⁹ *But the way of the wicked is like complete darkness. Those who follow it have no idea what they are stumbling over.*

²⁰ *Pay attention, my child, to what I say. Listen carefully.* ²¹ *Don't lose sight of my words. Let them penetrate deep within your heart,* ²² *for they bring life and radiant health to anyone who discovers their meaning.*

²³ *Above all else, guard your heart, for it affects everything you do.*

²⁴ *Avoid all perverse talk; stay far from corrupt speech.*

²⁵ *Look straight ahead, and fix your eyes on what lies before you.* ²⁶ *Mark out a straight path for your feet; then stick to the path and stay safe.* ²⁷ *Don't get sidetracked; keep your feet from following evil.*

Prayer: Lord, I know that self–control is the best form of control. However, I am weak, and I cannot do it by myself. Please give me the strength to control my desires. Help me to guard the things coming into my ears and eyes so that I am not distracted. Help me to walk in the Spirit and not give into my lower nature. Please give me strength to have victory in my life so that I can be a blessing to others. In Jesus' Name I pray, Amen.

Teachers are more than any other class the guardians of civilization. (Bertrand Russell)

Men learn while they teach. (Seneca)

Proverbs 5
Wisdom Instructs about Sexuality

Avoid Immoral Women

[1] *My son, pay attention to my wisdom; listen carefully to my wise counsel.* [2] *Then you will learn to be discreet and will store up knowledge.*

[3] *The lips of an immoral woman are as sweet as honey, and her mouth is smoother than oil.* [4] *But*

Pearl of Wisdom

307. Your most important mentor is the one you listen to and follow (Prov. 5:1–2). In life, you'll need more than one mentor.

the result is as bitter as poison, sharp as a double–edged sword. ⁵ *Her feet go down to death; her steps lead straight to the grave.* ⁶ *For she does not care about the path to life. She staggers down a crooked trail and doesn't even realize where it leads.*

⁷ *So now, my sons, listen to me. Never stray from what I am about to say:* ⁸ *Run from her! Don't go near the door of her house!* ⁹ *If you do, you will lose your honor and hand over to merciless people everything you have achieved in life.* ¹⁰ *Strangers will obtain your wealth, and someone else will enjoy the fruit of your labor.* ¹¹ *Afterward you will groan in anguish when disease consumes your body,* ¹² *and you will say, "How I hated discipline! If only I had not demanded my own way!* ¹³ *Oh, why didn't I listen to my teachers? Why didn't I pay attention to those who gave me instruction?* ¹⁴ *I have come to the brink of utter ruin, and now I must face public disgrace."*

¹⁵ *Drink water from your own well – share your love only with your wife.* ¹⁶ *Why spill the water of your springs in public, having sex with just anyone?* ¹⁷ *You should reserve it for yourselves. Don't share it with strangers.*

Pearls of Wisdom

1082. Instead of looking for greener pastures, water your own grass (Prov. 5:15–19).

269. Make your family your foundation and fountain of inspiration in life (Prov. 5:18).

---

¹⁸ *Let your wife be a fountain of blessing for you. Rejoice in the wife of your youth.* ¹⁹ *She is a loving doe, a graceful deer. Let her breasts satisfy you always. May you always be captivated by her love.* ²⁰ *Why be captivated, my son,*

with an immoral woman, or embrace the breasts of an adulterous woman?

[21] *For the LORD sees clearly what a man does, examining every path he takes.* [22] *An evil man is held captive by his own sins; they are ropes that catch and hold him.* [23] *He will die for lack of self–control; he will be lost because of his incredible folly.*

Prayer: I know that sex isn't evil because you created it. I realize that I'm not supposed to have sex outside of marriage. Help me to practice abstinence. When I do get married, please help me to be faithful to my partner. If I get weak and cannot seem to control myself, teach me to rely on your power. Father, with your help I know that I can have victory in this area of my life. Help me to stay pure and if I fall, please give me the strength to admit it and quit it. Lord, this is my sincere prayer in Jesus' Name. Amen.

The mere imparting of information is not education. Above all things, the effort must result in making a man think and do for himself. (Carter G. Woodson)

Education is helping the child realize his potentialities. (Erich Fromm)

Knowledge is proud that he has learned so much; wisdom is humble that he knows no more. (William Cowper)

I do not think much of a man who is not wiser today than he was yesterday. (Abraham Lincoln)

Proverbs 6

Wisdom Warns of Pitfalls to Avoid

Lessons for Daily Life

[1] *My child, if you co–sign a loan for a friend or guarantee the debt of someone you hardly know –* [2] *if you have trapped yourself by your agreement and are caught by what you said –* [3] *quick, get out of it if you possibly can! You have placed yourself at your friend's mercy. Now swallow your pride; go and beg to have your name erased.* [4] *Don't put it off. Do it now! Don't rest until you do.* [5] *Save yourself like a deer escaping from a hunter, like a bird fleeing from a net.*

[6] *Take a lesson from the ants, you lazybones. Learn from their ways and be wise!* [7] *Even though they have no prince, governor, or ruler to make them work,* [8] *they labor hard all summer, gathering food for the winter.* [9] *But you, lazybones, how long will you sleep? When will you wake up? I want you to*

Pearls of Wisdom

485. Planning and preparation will make you powerful and productive (Prov. 6:6–8).

774. Plan your time wisely and stick with your plan (Prov. 6:6–8).

1005. Spend less than you make and invest the rest (Prov. 6:6–8). Work for your money and then let your money work for you.

learn this lesson: ¹⁰ *A little extra sleep, a little more slumber, a little folding of the hands to rest –* ¹¹ *and poverty will pounce on you like a bandit; scarcity will attack you like an armed robber.*

¹² *Here is a description of worthless and wicked people: They*

Pearls of Wisdom

920. The best luck in the world is to get up off of your butt and do something with your life (Prov. 6:9–11).

55. After you get through dreaming, wake up and get busy making your dream come true (Prov. 6:10–11).

---

are constant liars, ¹³ *signaling their true intentions to their friends by making signs with their eyes and feet and fingers.* ¹⁴ *Their perverted hearts plot evil. They stir up trouble constantly.* ¹⁵ *But they will be destroyed suddenly, broken beyond all hope of healing.*

¹⁶ *There are six things the LORD hates – no, seven things he detests:*

¹⁷ *haughty eyes, a lying tongue, hands that kill the innocent,*

¹⁸ *a heart that plots evil, feet that race to do wrong,*

¹⁹ *a false witness who pours out lies, a person who sows discord among brothers.*

²⁰ *My son, obey your father's commands, and don't neglect your mother's teaching.* ²¹ *Keep their words always in your heart. Tie them around your neck.* ²² *Wherever you walk, their counsel can lead you. When you sleep, they will protect you. When you wake up in the morning, they will advise you.* ²³ *For these commands and this teaching are*

a lamp to light the way ahead of you. The correction of discipline is the way to life.

²⁴ These commands and this teaching will keep you from the immoral woman, from the smooth tongue of an adulterous woman. ²⁵ Don't lust for her beauty. Don't let her coyness seduce you. ²⁶ For a prostitute will bring you to poverty, and sleeping with another man's wife may cost you your very life. ²⁷ Can a man scoop fire into his lap and not be burned? ²⁸ Can he walk on hot coals and not blister his feet? ²⁹ So it is with the man who sleeps with another man's wife. He who embraces her will not go unpunished.

³⁰ Excuses might be found for a thief who steals because he is starving. ³¹ But if he is caught, he will be fined seven times as much as he stole, even if it means selling everything in his house to pay it back.

³² But the man who commits adultery is an utter fool, for he destroys his own soul. ³³ Wounds and constant disgrace are his lot. His shame will never be erased. ³⁴ For the woman's husband will be furious in his jealousy, and he will have no mercy in his day of vengeance. ³⁵ There is no compensation or bribe that will satisfy him.

Pearls of Wisdom

688. Habits are formed through discipline (Prov. 6:23).

436. What you see and hear determine what you think and feel and what you think and feel will determine what you will say and do (Prov. 6:25).

198. Everything nice in life has its price (Prov. 6:32–35).

Prayer: Lord, I realize that life is filled with temptations and traps. I know that the enemy of my soul is looking for an opportunity to trick me into doing something wrong. However, I don't have to become a victim, because I have victory in you. Lord, help me to see the pitfalls in my path and give me the power to go around them. As I study your Word, I know you will help me to stay on the straight and narrow path. Lord, this is my prayer for guidance in Jesus' Name, Amen.

Experience is a hard teacher. She gives the test first, and the lesson afterwards. (Author Unknown)

If you think education is expensive, try ignorance.
(Derek Bok)

Proverbs 7
Wisdom Warns against Fornication

Another Warning about Immoral Women

[1] *Follow my advice, my son; always treasure my commands.*
[2] *Obey them and live! Guard my teachings as your most precious possession.* [3] *Tie them on your fingers as a reminder. Write them deep within your heart.*

[4] *Love wisdom like a sister; make insight a beloved member of your family.* [5] *Let them hold you back from an affair with*

an immoral woman, from listening to the flattery of an adulterous woman.

⁶ *I was looking out the window of my house one day* ⁷ *and saw a simpleminded young man who lacked common sense.* ⁸ *He was crossing the street near the house of an immoral woman. He was strolling down the path by her house* ⁹ *at twilight, as the day was fading, as the dark of night set in.* ¹⁰ *The woman approached him, dressed seductively and sly of heart.* ¹¹ *She was the brash, rebellious type who never stays at home.* ¹² *She is often seen in the streets and markets, soliciting at every corner.*

¹³ *She threw her arms around him and kissed him, and with a brazen look she said,* ¹⁴ *"I've offered my sacrifices and just finished my vows.* ¹⁵ *It's you I was looking for! I came out to find you, and here you are!* ¹⁶ *My bed is spread with colored sheets of finest linen imported from Egypt.* ¹⁷ *I've perfumed my bed with myrrh, aloes, and cinnamon.* ¹⁸ *Come, let's drink our fill of love until morning. Let's enjoy each other's caresses,* ¹⁹ *for my husband is not home. He's away on a long trip.* ²⁰ *He has taken a wallet full of money with him, and he won't return until later in the month."*

²¹ *So she seduced him with her pretty speech. With her flattery she enticed him.* ²² *He followed her at once, like an ox going to the slaughter or like a trapped stag,* ²³ *awaiting the arrow that would pierce its heart. He was like a bird flying into a snare, little knowing it would cost him his life.*

Pearl of Wisdom

503. Your mind is the command and control center of your life (Prov. 7:1–27). What happens in your mind will happen in time.

---

24 Listen to me, my sons, and pay attention to my words.
25 Don't let your hearts stray away toward her. Don't wander down her wayward path. 26 For she has been the ruin of many; numerous men have been her victims. 27 Her house is the road to the grave. Her bedroom is the den of death.

Prayer: Lord, I realize that there is temptation around me at every turn. Please help me to monitor what I see and what I hear so that sexual thoughts won't get imbedded in my mind. Help me to stay in your Word because your Word will keep my mind pure. I know that if I can keep a pure mind, I can have a great life. Thank you for your keeping power. In Jesus' Name I pray, Amen.

The philosophy of the school room in one generation will be the philosophy of government in the next. (Abraham Lincoln, 1809-1865; 16th U.S. President, 1861-65)

Proverbs 8
Wisdom Proclaims Her Worth, Availability, and Accomplishments

<u>Wisdom Calls for a Hearing</u>

1 Listen as wisdom calls out! Hear as understanding raises her voice! 2 She stands on the hilltop and at the crossroads. 3 At the entrance to the city, at the city gates, she cries aloud, 4 "I call to you, to all of you! I am raising my voice to all people. [5] How naive you are! Let me give you common sense. O foolish ones, let me give you understanding. [6] Listen to me! For I have excellent things to tell you. Everything I say is right, [7] for I speak the truth and hate every kind of deception. [8] My advice is wholesome and good. There is nothing crooked or twisted in it. [9] My words are plain to anyone with understanding, clear to those who want to learn.

[10] *"Choose my instruction rather than silver, and knowledge over pure gold. [11] For wisdom is far more valuable than rubies. Nothing you desire can be compared with it.*

[12] *"I, Wisdom, live together with good judgment. I know where to discover knowledge and discernment. [13] All who fear the LORD will hate evil. That is why I hate pride, arrogance, corruption, and perverted speech. [14] Good advice and success belong to me. Insight and strength are mine. [15] Because of me, kings reign, and rulers make just laws. [16] Rulers lead with my help, and nobles make righteous judgments.*

Pearls of Wisdom

473. If God gives you an idea, He will make it real (Prov. 8:12).

548. Your mind is your gold mine (Prov. 8:12). It is priceless!

14. You won't stumble, fumble or crumble if you learn to stay humble (1 Cor. 10:12; Dan. 4:37; Prov. 8:13).

438. It is never right to do wrong (Prov. 8:13; Rom. 6:23).

998. If you avoid evil, it's a good chance that evil will avoid you (Prov. 8:13; 1 Thes. 5:22).

640. A little wisdom can obtain a lot of wealth (Prov. 8:18).

---

¹⁷ *"I love all who love me. Those who search for me will surely find me.* ¹⁸ *Unending riches, honor, wealth, and justice are mine to distribute.* ¹⁹ *My gifts are better than the purest gold, my wages better than sterling silver!* ²⁰ *I walk in righteousness, in paths of justice.* ²¹ *Those who love me inherit wealth, for I fill their treasuries.*

²² *"The LORD formed me from the beginning, before he created anything else.* ²³ *I was appointed in ages past, at the very first, before the earth began.* ²⁴ *I was born before the oceans were created, before the springs bubbled forth their waters.* ²⁵ *Before the mountains and the hills were formed, I was born –* ²⁶ *before he had made the earth and fields and the first handfuls of soil.*

²⁷ *"I was there when he established the heavens, when he drew the horizon on the oceans.* ²⁸ *I was there when he set the clouds above, when he established the deep fountains of the earth.* ²⁹ *I was there when he set the limits of the seas, so they would not spread beyond their boundaries. And when he marked off the earth's foundations,* ³⁰ *I was the architect at his side. I was his constant delight, rejoicing always in his presence.* ³¹ *And how happy I was with what he created – his wide world and all the human family!*

Pearl of Wisdom

206. To expedite your success, listen more and talk less (Prov. 8:33–34).

---

³² *"And so, my children, listen to me, for happy are all who follow my ways.* ³³ *Listen to my counsel and be wise. Don't ignore it.*

³⁴ *"Happy are those who listen to me, watching for me daily at my gates, waiting for me outside my home!* ³⁵ *For whoever finds me finds life and wins approval from the*

LORD. ³⁶ *But those who miss me have injured themselves. All who hate me love death."*

Prayer: Lord, I realize your wisdom is available to all who ask. I realize the value of wisdom. I know it is more valuable than anything on earth I could possibly want. I know that it is through your wisdom that I can get all the other worthwhile things in life. I ask you to give me the master key of wisdom so I can be blessed as well as be a blessing to others. For this is my prayer in Jesus' Name, Amen.

Proverbs 9
Wisdom Spreads a Banquet and Gives Instructions

¹ *Wisdom has built her spacious house with seven pillars.* ² *She has prepared a great banquet, mixed the wines, and set the table.* ³ *She has sent her servants to invite everyone to come. She calls out from the heights overlooking the city.* ⁴ *"Come home with me," she urges the simple. To those without good judgment, she says,* ⁵ *"Come, eat my food, and drink the wine I have mixed.* ⁶ *Leave your foolish ways behind, and begin to live; learn how to be wise."*

⁷ *Anyone who rebukes a mocker will get a smart retort. Anyone who rebukes the wicked will get hurt.* ⁸ *So don't bother rebuking mockers; they will only hate you. But the wise, when rebuked, will love you all the more.* ⁹ *Teach the wise, and they will be wiser. Teach the righteous, and they will learn more.*

¹⁰ Fear of the LORD is the beginning of wisdom. Knowledge of the Holy One results in understanding.

¹¹ Wisdom will multiply your days and add years to your life. ¹² If you become wise, you will be the one to benefit. If you scorn wisdom, you will be the one to suffer.

Folly Calls for a Hearing

¹³ The woman named Folly is loud and brash. She is ignorant and doesn't even know it. ¹⁴ She sits in her doorway on the heights overlooking the city. ¹⁵ She calls out to men going by who are minding their own business. ¹⁶ "Come home with me," she urges the simple. To those without good judgment, she says, ¹⁷ "Stolen water is refreshing; food eaten in secret tastes the best!" ¹⁸ But the men don't realize that her former guests are now in the grave.

Prayer: Lord, help me to listen to your instructions so that I will be wise. I want to build my life upon the seven pillars of wisdom. I know that a holy reverence of you is the first step in gaining wisdom and understanding. I know that wisdom will help me successfully navigate my way safely through the pitfalls of life. I cannot make this journey through life successfully without you. Please lead and guide me. For this is my prayer in Jesus' Name, Amen.

Character cannot be developed in ease and quiet. Only through experiences of trial and suffering can the soul be strengthened, vision cleared, ambition inspired and success achieved. (Helen Keller)

Proverbs 10
Wisdom Instructs on Right and Wrong

The Proverbs of Solomon

¹ *A wise child brings joy to a father; a foolish child brings grief to a mother.*

² *Ill–gotten gain has no lasting value, but right living can save your life.*

³ *The LORD will not let the godly starve to death, but he refuses to satisfy the craving of the wicked.*

Pearls of Wisdom

52. It is better to work and get paid nothing than to get paid and do nothing (Prov. 10:4; 12:24; 13:4; 21:5).

519. Successful navigation requires thorough preparation (Ps. 37:5; Prov. 10:4).

575. It is easier to slow down a rabbit than to speed up a turtle (Prov. 10:4).

582. If you live life on the cutting edge, you will always be sharp and ahead of the pack (Prov. 10:4; 12:24; 13:4; 21:5).

966. If it was easy to be successful, then everyone would be successful (Prov. 10:4).

⁴ *Lazy people are soon poor; hard workers get rich.*

⁵ *A wise youth works hard all summer; a youth who sleeps away the hour of opportunity brings shame.*

⁶ *The godly are showered with blessings; evil people cover up their harmful intentions.*

⁷ *We all have happy memories of the godly, but the name of a wicked person rots away.*

⁸ *The wise are glad to be instructed, but babbling fools fall flat on their faces.*

⁹ *People with integrity have firm footing, but those who follow crooked paths will slip and fall.*

¹⁰ *People who wink at wrong cause trouble, but a bold reproof promotes peace.*

¹¹ *The words of the godly lead to life; evil people cover up their harmful intentions.*

¹² *Hatred stirs up quarrels, but love covers all offenses.*

¹³ *Wise words come from the lips of people with understanding, but fools will be punished with a rod.*

¹⁴ *Wise people treasure knowledge, but the babbling of a fool invites trouble.*

¹⁵ *The wealth of the rich is their fortress; the poverty of the poor is their calamity.*

¹⁶ *The earnings of the godly enhance their lives, but evil people squander their money on sin.*

¹⁷ *People who accept correction are on the pathway to life, but those who ignore it will lead others astray.*

¹⁸ *To hide hatred is to be a liar; to slander is to be a fool.*

Pearl of Wisdom

1090. The less you say the more people will remember (Prov. 10:19).

¹⁹ *Don't talk too much, for it fosters sin. Be sensible and turn off the flow!*

²⁰ *The words of the godly are like sterling silver; the heart of a fool is worthless.*

21 *The godly give good advice, but fools are destroyed by their lack of common sense.*

22 *The blessing of the LORD makes a person rich, and he adds no sorrow with it.*

Pearl of Wisdom

492. Grace is God's blessing and favor upon your life (Prov. 10:22).

---

23 *Doing wrong is fun for a fool, while wise conduct is a pleasure to the wise.*

24 *The fears of the wicked will all come true; so will the hopes of the godly.*

25 *Disaster strikes like a cyclone, whirling the wicked away, but the godly have a lasting foundation.*

26 *Lazy people are a pain to their employer. They are like smoke in the eyes or vinegar that sets the teeth on edge.*

27 *Fear of the LORD lengthens one's life, but the years of the wicked are cut short.*

28 *The hopes of the godly result in happiness, but the expectations of the wicked are all in vain.*

29 *The LORD protects the upright but destroys the wicked.*

30 *The godly will never be disturbed, but the wicked will be removed from the land.*

31 *The godly person gives wise advice, but the tongue that deceives will be cut off.*

32 *The godly speak words that are helpful, but the wicked speak only what is corrupt.*

Prayer: Lord, I know the pathway to your blessing is obedience. I ask that you help me to do the right thing. I know that I can live in the fullness of your blessings if I live right. I ask for your wisdom and power to put into practice the things I've learned so that I can be successful in every area of my life. Father, I give you thanks for all the things you have blessed me with already. I am so grateful! In Jesus' Name I pray, Amen.

Teaching is the royal road to learning. (Jessamyn West)

What we have to learn to do, we learn by doing. (Aristotle)

To teach is to touch lives forever. (Anonymous)

Setting an example is not the main means of influencing another, it is the only means. (Albert Einstein)

Education is not preparation for life; education is life itself. (John Dewey)

To talk in public, to think in solitude, to read and to hear, to inquire and answer inquiries, is the business of the scholar. (Samuel Johnson)

Books are the best of things, well used; abused, among the worst. What is the right use? What is the one end, which all means go to effect? They are for nothing but to inspire. (Ralph Waldo Emerson, 1803-1882, American Poet, Essayist)

Proverbs 11
Wisdom Avoids All Kinds of Wickedness

[1] *The LORD hates cheating, but he delights in honesty.*

[2] *Pride leads to disgrace, but with humility comes wisdom.*

[3] *Good people are guided by their honesty; treacherous people are destroyed by their dishonesty.*

[4] *Riches won't help on the day of judgment, but right living is a safeguard against death.*

[5] *The godly are directed by their honesty; the wicked fall beneath their load of sin.*

[6] *The godliness of good people rescues them; the ambition of treacherous people traps them.*

[7] *When the wicked die, their hopes all perish, for they rely on their own feeble strength.*

[8] *God rescues the godly from danger, but he lets the wicked fall into trouble.*

[9] *Evil words destroy one's friends; wise discernment rescues the godly.*

[10] *The whole city celebrates when the godly succeed; they shout for joy when the godless die.*

[11] *Upright citizens bless a city and make it prosper, but the talk of the wicked tears it apart.*

[12] *It is foolish to belittle a neighbor; a person with good sense remains silent.*

[13] *A gossip goes around revealing secrets, but those who are trustworthy can keep a confidence.*

[14] *Without wise leadership, a nation falls; with many counselors, there is safety.*

[15] *Guaranteeing a loan for a stranger is dangerous; it is better to refuse than to suffer later.*

[16] *Beautiful women obtain wealth, and violent men get rich.*

[17] *Your own soul is nourished when you are kind, but you destroy yourself when you are cruel.*

[18] *Evil people get rich for the moment, but the reward of the godly will last.*

[19] *Godly people find life; evil people find death.*

[20] *The LORD hates people with twisted hearts, but he delights in those who have integrity.*

[21] *You can be sure that evil people will be punished, but the children of the godly will go free.*

²² *A woman who is beautiful but lacks discretion is like a gold ring in a pig's snout.*

²³ *The godly can look forward to happiness, while the wicked can expect only wrath.*

²⁴ *It is possible to give freely and become more wealthy, but those who are stingy will lose everything.*

²⁵ *The generous prosper and are satisfied; those who refresh others will themselves be refreshed.*

²⁶ *People curse those who hold their grain for higher prices, but they bless the one who sells to them in their time of need.*

²⁷ *If you search for good, you will find favor; but if you search for evil, it will find you!*

Pearls of Wisdom

565. Giving is the highest form of living (Prov. 11:25; Acts 20:35).

691. Be wise and help those who have gone astray find their way (Prov. 11:30; Dan. 12:3).

---

²⁸ *Trust in your money and down you go! But the godly flourish like leaves in spring.*

²⁹ *Those who bring trouble on their families inherit only the wind. The fool will be a servant to the wise.*

³⁰ *The godly are like trees that bear life–giving fruit, and those who save lives are wise.*

³¹ *If the righteous are rewarded here on earth, how much more true that the wicked and the sinner will get what they deserve!*

Prayer: Lord, I ask for advice from you because you are the source of all truth. I also ask you to give me wise and understanding friends. I want to be a blessing to my friends as well by giving them sound advice. I ask that you help me stay out of trouble and help me to help my friends as well. When I do make a mistake, I ask that you would forgive me and give me another chance. Lord, I thank you for being a God of love and mercy. In Jesus' Name I pray, Amen.

Theories and goals of education don't matter a whit if you don't consider your students to be human beings. (Lou Ann Walker)

We cannot always build the future for our youth, but we can build our youth for the future. (Franklin D. Roosevelt)

Anyone who stops learning is old, whether at twenty or eighty. Anyone who keeps learning stays young. The greatest thing in life is to keep your mind young. (Henry Ford)

Learn as though you would never be able to master it; hold it as though you would be in fear of losing it. (Confucius)

The will to succeed is important, but what's even more important is the will to prepare. (Bobby Knight)

A good head and a good heart are always a formidable combination. (Nelson Mandela)

Proverbs 12
Wisdom Contrasts Righteousness and Wickedness

[1] *To learn, you must love discipline; it is stupid to hate correction.*

[2] *The LORD approves of those who are good, but he condemns those who plan wickedness.*

[3] *Wickedness never brings stability; only the godly have deep roots.*

[4] *A worthy wife is her husband's joy and crown; a shameful wife saps his strength.*

[5] *The plans of the godly are just; the advice of the wicked is treacherous.*

[6] *The words of the wicked are like a murderous ambush, but the words of the godly save lives.*

[7] *The wicked perish and are gone, but the children of the godly stand firm.*

[8] *Everyone admires a person with good sense, but a warped mind is despised.*

[9] *It is better to be a nobody with a servant than to be self-important but have no food.*

[10] *The godly are concerned for the welfare of their animals, but even the kindness of the wicked is cruel.*

[11] *Hard work means prosperity; only fools idle away their time.*

¹² *Thieves are jealous of each other's loot, while the godly bear their own fruit.*

¹³ *The wicked are trapped by their own words, but the godly escape such trouble.*

¹⁴ *People can get many good things by the words they say; the work of their hands also gives them many benefits.*

¹⁵ *Fools think they need no advice, but the wise listen to others.*

¹⁶ *A fool is quick–tempered, but a wise person stays calm when insulted.*

¹⁷ *An honest witness tells the truth; a false witness tells lies.*

Pearls of Wisdom

29. He who thinks he knows everything is a fool (Prov. 12:15).

118. Fight for feedback and if it's valid, follow it (Prov. 12:15).

¹⁸ *Some people make cutting remarks, but the words of the wise bring healing.*

¹⁹ *Truth stands the test of time; lies are soon exposed.*

²⁰ *Deceit fills hearts that are plotting evil; joy fills hearts that are planning peace!*

²¹ *No real harm befalls the godly, but the wicked have their fill of trouble.*

²² *The LORD hates those who don't keep their word, but he delights in those who do.*

²³ *Wise people don't make a show of their knowledge, but fools broadcast their folly.*

²⁴ *Work hard and become a leader; be lazy and become a slave.*

²⁵ *Worry weighs a person down; an encouraging word cheers a person up.*

²⁶ *The godly give good advice to their friends; the wicked lead them astray.*

²⁷ *Lazy people don't even cook the game they catch, but the diligent make use of everything they find.*

²⁸ *The way of the godly leads to life; their path does not lead to death.*

Prayer: Lord, I thank you for giving me discretion and discernment so I can distinguish between right and wrong. Please give me the strength to choose the right path. Even though I know what is right in my head, help me to do what is right deep down in my heart. I trust your power in me to do the right thing at all times. Keep me on the path of righteousness in Jesus' Name I pray. Amen.

Nothing in all the world is more dangerous than sincere ignorance and conscientious stupidity.
(Dr. Martin Luther King, Jr.)

Education has for its object the formation of character.
(Herbert Spencer, 1820-1903,
English Philosopher, Naturalist)

Learn from examples in history lest thou
be made an example. (John Boys)

Proverbs 13
Wisdom Instructs on Right Living

¹ *A wise child accepts a parent's discipline; a young mocker refuses to listen.*

² *Good people enjoy the positive results of their words, but those who are treacherous crave violence.*

³ *Those who control their tongue will have a long life; a quick retort can ruin everything.*

⁴ *Lazy people want much but get little, but those who work hard will prosper and be satisfied.*

⁵ *Those who are godly hate lies; the wicked come to shame and disgrace.*

⁶ *Godliness helps people all through life, while the evil are destroyed by their wickedness.*

⁷ *Some who are poor pretend to be rich; others who are rich pretend to be poor.*

⁸ *The rich can pay a ransom, but the poor won't even get threatened.*

⁹ *The life of the godly is full of light and joy, but the sinner's light is snuffed out.*

¹⁰ *Pride leads to arguments; those who take advice are wise.*

¹¹ *Wealth from get–rich–quick schemes quickly disappears; wealth from hard work grows.*

¹² *Hope deferred makes the heart sick, but when dreams come true, there is life and joy.*

¹³ People who despise advice will find themselves in trouble; those who respect it will succeed.

¹⁴ The advice of the wise is like a life–giving fountain; those who accept it avoid the snares of death.

¹⁵ A person with good sense is respected; a treacherous person walks a rocky road.

¹⁶ Wise people think before they act; fools don't and even brag about it!

¹⁷ An unreliable messenger stumbles into trouble, but a reliable messenger brings healing.

¹⁸ If you ignore criticism, you will end in poverty and disgrace; if you accept criticism, you will be honored.

¹⁹ It is pleasant to see dreams come true, but fools will not turn from evil to attain them.

²⁰ Whoever walks with the wise will become wise; whoever walks with fools will suffer harm.

Pearls of Wisdom

437. God is against sin because sin is against you (Prov. 13:15).

114. Birds of a feather do flock together (Prov. 13:20).

1016. The law of attractions says, you attract who you are not who you want (Prov. 13:20).

²¹ Trouble chases sinners, while blessings chase the righteous!

²² Good people leave an inheritance to their grandchildren, but the sinner's wealth passes to the godly.

²³ A poor person's farm may produce much food, but injustice sweeps it all away.

²⁴ *If you refuse to discipline your children, it proves you don't love them; if you love your children, you will be prompt to discipline them.*

²⁵ *The godly eat to their hearts' content, but the belly of the wicked goes hungry.*

Prayer: Lord, as I start my day I pray that you will help me to keep your Word in my heart so that I might not sin against you. I acknowledge you in all my ways and I will obey you all of my days. I will walk in your wisdom and share your wisdom with others. Lord, give me sanctified common sense in all things so that I can live for your glory. This is my prayer in Jesus' Name. Amen.

The secret of education is respecting the pupil.
(Ralph Waldo Emerson)

Proverbs 14
Wisdom Instructs about the Fear of the Lord

¹ *A wise woman builds her house; a foolish woman tears hers down with her own hands.*

² *Those who follow the right path fear the LORD; those who take the wrong path despise him.*

³ *The talk of fools is a rod for their backs, but the words of the wise keep them out of trouble.*

⁴ An empty stable stays clean, but no income comes from an empty stable.

⁵ A truthful witness does not lie; a false witness breathes lies.

⁶ A mocker seeks wisdom and never finds it, but knowledge comes easily to those with understanding.

⁷ Stay away from fools, for you won't find knowledge there.

⁸ The wise look ahead to see what is coming, but fools deceive themselves.

⁹ Fools make fun of guilt, but the godly acknowledge it and seek reconciliation.

¹⁰ Each heart knows its own bitterness, and no one else can fully share its joy.

¹¹ The house of the wicked will perish, but the tent of the godly will flourish.

Pearl of Wisdom

1085. Being gay is not the way even though society says it's okay (Lev. 18:22; Prov. 14:12; Rom. 1:24-27).

---

¹² There is a path before each person that seems right, but it ends in death.

¹³ Laughter can conceal a heavy heart; when the laughter ends, the grief remains.

¹⁴ Backsliders get what they deserve; good people receive their reward.

¹⁵ Only simpletons believe everything they are told! The prudent carefully consider their steps.

¹⁶ The wise are cautious and avoid danger; fools plunge ahead with great confidence.

17 Those who are short–tempered do foolish things, and schemers are hated.

18 The simpleton is clothed with folly, but the wise person is crowned with knowledge.

19 Evil people will bow before good people; the wicked will bow at the gates of the godly.

20 The poor are despised even by their neighbors, while the rich have many "friends."

21 It is sin to despise one's neighbors; blessed are those who help the poor.

Pearls of Wisdom

368. Planning makes you powerful. People follow the man or woman who has a plan (Prov. 14:22).

177. He who talks much does very little (Prov. 14:23).

381. Nothing happens until people start talking. And if all they do is talk nothing still will happen (Prov. 14:23).

---

22 If you plot evil, you will be lost; but if you plan good, you will be granted unfailing love and faithfulness.

23 Work brings profit, but mere talk leads to poverty!

24 Wealth is a crown for the wise; the effort of fools yields only folly.

25 A truthful witness saves lives, but a false witness is a traitor.

26 Those who fear the LORD are secure; he will be a place of refuge for their children.

27 Fear of the LORD is a life–giving fountain; it offers escape from the snares of death.

[28] *A growing population is a king's glory; a dwindling nation is his doom.*

[29] *Those who control their anger have great understanding; those with a hasty temper will make mistakes.*

[30] *A relaxed attitude lengthens life; jealousy rots it away.*

[31] *Those who oppress the poor insult their Maker, but those who help the poor honor him.*

[32] *The wicked are crushed by their sins, but the godly have a refuge when they die.*

[33] *Wisdom is enshrined in an understanding heart; wisdom is not found among fools.*

[34] *Godliness exalts a nation, but sin is a disgrace to any people.*

[35] *A king rejoices in servants who know what they are doing; he is angry with those who cause trouble.*

Pearl of Wisdom

399. Sin always dishonors God and discredits the leader (Prov. 14:34), but God's grace can give you another chance (1 John 1:9).

Prayer: Lord, I reverence and respect you as my God. I honor you for your holiness and righteousness. I thank you for your goodness and mercy towards me. Help me to live a life that is pleasing in your sight. Help me not to follow the path of the world but to follow your righteous precepts so that I will be blessed in every area of my life. As you bless me, please make me a blessing to others. This is my prayer in Jesus' Name. Amen.

Proverbs 15

Wisdom Instructs on Right Emotions and the Right Way to Live

¹ *A gentle answer turns away wrath, but harsh words stir up anger.*

² *The wise person makes learning a joy; fools spout only foolishness.*

Pearl of Wisdom

1006. Nobody resents kind words (Prov. 15:1).

³ *The LORD is watching everywhere, keeping his eye on both the evil and the good.*

⁴ *Gentle words bring life and health; a deceitful tongue crushes the spirit.*

⁵ *Only a fool despises a parent's discipline; whoever learns from correction is wise.*

⁶ *There is treasure in the house of the godly, but the earnings of the wicked bring trouble.*

⁷ *Only the wise can give good advice; fools cannot do so.*

⁸ *The LORD hates the sacrifice of the wicked, but he delights in the prayers of the upright.*

⁹ *The LORD despises the way of the wicked, but he loves those who pursue godliness.*

¹⁰ *Whoever abandons the right path will be severely punished; whoever hates correction will die.*

¹¹ *Even the depths of Death and Destruction are known by the LORD. How much more does he know the human heart!*

¹² *Mockers don't love those who rebuke them, so they stay away from the wise.*

¹³ *A glad heart makes a happy face; a broken heart crushes the spirit.*

¹⁴ *A wise person is hungry for truth, while the fool feeds on trash.*

¹⁵ *For the poor, every day brings trouble; for the happy heart, life is a continual feast.*

Pearl of Wisdom

717. Happy people are usually the healthiest people (Prov. 15:13; 15:15; 17:22).

¹⁶ *It is better to have little with fear for the LORD than to have great treasure with turmoil.*

¹⁷ *A bowl of soup with someone you love is better than steak with someone you hate.*

¹⁸ *A hothead starts fights; a cool–tempered person tries to stop them.*

¹⁹ *A lazy person has trouble all through life; the path of the upright is easy!*

²⁰ *Sensible children bring joy to their father; foolish children despise their mother.*

²¹ *Foolishness brings joy to those who have no sense; a sensible person stays on the right path.*

²² *Plans go wrong for lack of advice; many counselors bring success.*

²³ *Everyone enjoys a fitting reply; it is wonderful to say the right thing at the right time!*

²⁴ *The path of the wise leads to life above; they leave the grave behind.*

²⁵ *The LORD destroys the house of the proud, but he protects the property of widows.*

²⁶ *The LORD despises the thoughts of the wicked, but he delights in pure words.*

²⁷ *Dishonest money brings grief to the whole family, but those who hate bribes will live.*

²⁸ *The godly think before speaking; the wicked spout evil words.*

²⁹ *The LORD is far from the wicked, but he hears the prayers of the righteous.*

³⁰ *A cheerful look brings joy to the heart; good news makes for good health.*

³¹ *If you listen to constructive criticism, you will be at home among the wise.*

³² *If you reject criticism, you only harm yourself; but if you listen to correction, you grow in understanding.*

³³ *Fear of the LORD teaches a person to be wise; humility precedes honor.*

Prayer: Lord, I commit my emotions to you. I want to be whole and healthy in every area of my life. Help me to guard my heart so that I can control my emotions. Help me to take care of my body. Help me to keep my spirit focused on you. Help me to keep my mind clean by putting the right things into it on a daily basis. I ask you to help me to be balanced as your child. I pray all of this in Jesus' Name. Amen.

Proverbs 16
Wisdom Instructs on God's Providential Care

[1] *We can gather our thoughts, but the LORD gives the right answer.*

[2] *People may be pure in their own eyes, but the LORD examines their motives.*

[3] *Commit your work to the LORD, and then your plans will succeed.*

[4] *The LORD has made everything for his own purposes, even the wicked for punishment.*

[5] *The LORD despises pride; be assured that the proud will be punished.*

[6] *Unfailing love and faithfulness cover sin; evil is avoided by fear of the LORD.*

[7] *When the ways of people please the LORD, he makes even their enemies live at peace with them.*

[8] *It is better to be poor and godly than rich and dishonest.*

[9] *We can make our plans, but the LORD determines our steps.*

[10] *The king speaks with divine wisdom; he must never judge unfairly.*

¹¹ *The LORD demands fairness in every business deal; he sets the standard.*

¹² *A king despises wrongdoing, for his rule depends on his justice.*

¹³ *The king is pleased with righteous lips; he loves those who speak honestly.*

¹⁴ *The anger of the king is a deadly threat; the wise do what they can to appease it.*

¹⁵ *When the king smiles, there is life; his favor refreshes like a gentle rain.*

¹⁶ *How much better to get wisdom than gold, and understanding than silver!*

¹⁷ *The path of the upright leads away from evil; whoever follows that path is safe.*

¹⁸ *Pride goes before destruction, and haughtiness before a fall.*

¹⁹ *It is better to live humbly with the poor than to share plunder with the proud.*

Pearls of Wisdom

264. The Bible is still the all time best seller because its content is priceless (Ps. 19:10a; 119:127; Prov. 16:16).

385. Arrogant people are full of hot air. They are suffering from an acute case of big headedness (Prov. 16:18; 1 Tim. 3:6).

560. What's the middle letter in **Pride**? What is the middle letter in **Sin**? I **think** you get my **point** (Prov. 1618)!

---

²⁰ *Those who listen to instruction will prosper; those who trust the LORD will be happy.*

21 *The wise are known for their understanding, and instruction is appreciated if it's well presented.*

22 *Discretion is a life–giving fountain to those who possess it, but discipline is wasted on fools.*

23 *From a wise mind comes wise speech; the words of the wise are persuasive.*

24 *Kind words are like honey – sweet to the soul and healthy for the body.*

25 *There is a path before each person that seems right, but it ends in death.*

26 *It is good for workers to have an appetite; an empty stomach drives them on.*

27 *Scoundrels hunt for scandal; their words are a destructive blaze.*

28 *A troublemaker plants seeds of strife; gossip separates the best of friends.*

29 *Violent people deceive their companions, leading them down a harmful path.*

30 *With narrowed eyes, they plot evil; without a word, they plan their mischief.*

31 *Gray hair is a crown of glory; it is gained by living a godly life.*

32 *It is better to be patient than powerful; it is better to have self–control than to conquer a city.*

Pearls of Wisdom

87. The best control in the world is self–control (Prov. 16:32).

569. The only person you have any real control over is you so stop being frustrated by the crazy stuff people do (Prov. 16:32).

[33] We may throw the dice, but the LORD determines how they fall.

Prayer: Lord, I commit my day and my way to you. I want to start today by giving you my devotion. I ask for your guidance today as I go forward with my agenda. I pray that your agenda will be my agenda. I don't want to do anything that's not pleasing to you. I want to acknowledge you in all that I do. I want to walk in your wisdom and make good decisions. I need your power, protection and provision. After today is over I promise to give you the praise. This I pray in Jesus' Name. Amen.

The goal of education is the advancement of knowledge and the dissemination of truths. (John F. Kennedy)

Sixty years ago I knew everything; now I know nothing; education is a progressive discovery of our own ignorance. (Will Durant)

Life is a festival only to the wise. (Ralph Waldo Emerson)

One good head is better than a hundred strong hands. (Thomas Fuller)

On one occasion Aristotle was asked how much educated men were superior to those uneducated; "As much," said he, "as the living are to the dead." (Diogenes Laertius)

Proverbs 17
Wisdom Instructs on Fools

¹ *A dry crust eaten in peace is better than a great feast with strife.*

² *A wise slave will rule over the master's shameful sons and will share their inheritance.*

³ *Fire tests the purity of silver and gold, but the LORD tests the heart.*

⁴ *Wrongdoers listen to wicked talk; liars pay attention to destructive words.*

⁵ *Those who mock the poor insult their Maker; those who rejoice at the misfortune of others will be punished.*

⁶ *Grandchildren are the crowning glory of the aged; parents are the pride of their children.*

⁷ *Eloquent speech is not fitting for a fool; even less are lies fitting for a ruler.*

⁸ *A bribe seems to work like magic for those who give it; they succeed in all they do.*

⁹ *Disregarding another person's faults preserves love; telling about them separates close friends.*

¹⁰ *A single rebuke does more for a person of understanding than a hundred lashes on the back of a fool.*

¹¹ *Evil people seek rebellion, but they will be severely punished.*

¹² *It is safer to meet a bear robbed of her cubs than to confront a fool caught in folly.*

¹³ *If you repay evil for good, evil will never leave your house.*

¹⁴ *Beginning a quarrel is like opening a floodgate, so drop the matter before a dispute breaks out.*

¹⁵ *The LORD despises those who acquit the guilty and condemn the innocent.*

¹⁶ *It is senseless to pay tuition to educate a fool who has no heart for wisdom.*

¹⁷ *A friend is always loyal, and a brother is born to help in time of need.*

¹⁸ *It is poor judgment to co-sign a friend's note, to become responsible for a neighbor's debts.*

¹⁹ *Anyone who loves to quarrel loves sin; anyone who speaks boastfully invites disaster.*

²⁰ *The crooked heart will not prosper; the twisted tongue tumbles into trouble.*

²¹ *It is painful to be the parent of a fool; there is no joy for the father of a rebel.*

²² *A cheerful heart is good medicine, but a broken spirit saps a person's strength.*

Pearls of Wisdom

1099. Laughter is good medicine for the soul (Prov. 17:22).

303. He who laughs lives long enough to laugh again and again (Prov. 17:22a).

462. It's not so much what you eat that will affect your health as what's eating you (Prov. 17:22b).

²³ *The wicked accept secret bribes to pervert justice.*

²⁴ *Sensible people keep their eyes glued on wisdom, but a fool's eyes wander to the ends of the earth.*

²⁵ *A foolish child brings grief to a father and bitterness to a mother.*

²⁶ *It is wrong to fine the godly for being good or to punish nobles for being honest!*

²⁷ *A truly wise person uses few words; a person with understanding is even–tempered.*

Pearl of Wisdom

891. A real friend knows all about you and still loves you (Prov. 17:27).

²⁸ *Even fools are thought to be wise when they keep silent; when they keep their mouths shut, they seem intelligent.*

Prayer: Lord, I know that trials and tribulations are part of life. I realize that this world isn't perfect. I also understand that people aren't perfect either, including me. I ask that you will give me your wisdom and power to deal with the challenges I face every day. I know that in the end you will make me better, stronger and a wiser person as a result of my current suffering. This is my prayer today in Jesus' Name. Amen.

People get wisdom from thinking not from learning.
(Laura Riding)

Proverbs 18

Wisdom Instructs on Moral Virtues
and Their Contrary Vices

[1] *A recluse is self–indulgent, snarling at every sound principle of conduct.*

[2] *Fools have no interest in understanding; they only want to air their own opinions.*

[3] *When the wicked arrive, contempt, shame, and disgrace are sure to follow.*

[4] *A person's words can be life–giving water; words of true wisdom are as refreshing as a bubbling brook.*

[5] *It is wrong for a judge to favor the guilty or condemn the innocent.*

[6] *Fools get into constant quarrels; they are asking for a beating.*

[7] *The mouths of fools are their ruin; their lips get them into trouble.*

[8] *What dainty morsels rumors are – but they sink deep into one's heart.*

[9] *A lazy person is as bad as someone who destroys things.*

[10] *The name of the LORD is a strong fortress; the godly run to him and are safe.*

[11] *The rich think of their wealth as an impregnable defense; they imagine it is a high wall of safety.*

[12] *Haughtiness goes before destruction; humility precedes honor.*

¹³ *What a shame, what folly, to give advice before listening to the facts!*

¹⁴ *The human spirit can endure a sick body, but who can bear it if the spirit is crushed?*

¹⁵ *Intelligent people are always open to new ideas. In fact, they look for them.*

¹⁶ *Giving a gift works wonders; it may bring you before important people!*

¹⁷ *Any story sounds true until someone sets the record straight.*

¹⁸ *Casting lots can end arguments and settle disputes between powerful opponents.*

Pearls of Wisdom

31. Your talent creates your treasure and your gifts create your gold in life (Prov. 18:16).

329. Talk about your positive expectations rather than your negative experiences (Prov. 18:21).

¹⁹ *It's harder to make amends with an offended friend than to capture a fortified city. Arguments separate friends like a gate locked with iron bars.*

²⁰ *Words satisfy the soul as food satisfies the stomach; the right words on a person's lips bring satisfaction.*

²¹ *Those who love to talk will experience the consequences, for the tongue can kill or nourish life.*

²² *The man who finds a wife finds a treasure and receives favor from the LORD.*

²³ *The poor plead for mercy; the rich answer with insults.*

24 *There are "friends" who destroy each other, but a real friend sticks closer than a brother.*

Prayer: Lord, I ask that I will have the courage to live out my convictions. I want to live a life of virtues and not vices. Help me to always remember that your way is the best way. Help me not to compromise in my daily decisions. Help me to walk upright and be a person of integrity. Help me to honor you in everything I say and do. I will give you the praise for your grace and goodness always. This I pray today in Jesus' Name. Amen.

Thoughts are energy. And you can make your world or break your world by thinking. (Susan Taylor)

Each time we re-read a book we get more out of it because we put more into it; a different person is reading it, and therefore it is a different book. (Muriel Clark)

Education is not the filling of a pail, but the lighting of a fire. (William Butler Yeats)

Knowledge is horizontal. Wisdom is vertical--comes down from above. (Billy Graham)

Proverbs 19

Wisdom Instructs on Character

[1] *It is better to be poor and honest than to be a fool and dishonest.*

[2] *Zeal without knowledge is not good; a person who moves too quickly may go the wrong way.*

[3] *People ruin their lives by their own foolishness and then are angry at the LORD.*

[4] *Wealth makes many "friends"; poverty drives them away.*

[5] *A false witness will not go unpunished, nor will a liar escape.*

[6] *Many beg favors from a prince; everyone is the friend of a person who gives gifts!*

[7] *If the relatives of the poor despise them, how much more will their friends avoid them. The poor call after them, but they are gone.*

[8] *To acquire wisdom is to love oneself; people who cherish understanding will prosper.*

[9] *A false witness will not go unpunished, and a liar will be destroyed.*

Pearl of Wisdom

169. A fish wouldn't get caught if he kept his mouth closed. Speech might be silver but silence is golden (Prov. 19:11).

[10] *It isn't right for a fool to live in luxury or for a slave to rule over princes!*

[11] *People with good sense restrain their anger; they earn esteem by overlooking wrongs.*

¹² *The king's anger is like a lion's roar, but his favor is like dew on the grass.*

¹³ *A foolish child is a calamity to a father; a nagging wife annoys like a constant dripping.*

¹⁴ *Parents can provide their sons with an inheritance of houses and wealth, but only the LORD can give an understanding wife.*

¹⁵ *A lazy person sleeps soundly – and goes hungry.*

¹⁶ *Keep the commandments and keep your life; despising them leads to death.*

¹⁷ *If you help the poor, you are lending to the LORD – and he will repay you!*

¹⁸ *Discipline your children while there is hope. If you don't, you will ruin their lives.*

¹⁹ *Short–tempered people must pay their own penalty. If you rescue them once, you will have to do it again.*

Pearl of Wisdom

201. The advice you heed will determine the life you lead (Prov. 19:20).

²⁰ *Get all the advice and instruction you can, and be wise the rest of your life.*

²¹ *You can make many plans, but the LORD's purpose will prevail.*

²² *Loyalty makes a person attractive. And it is better to be poor than dishonest.*

²³ *Fear of the LORD gives life, security, and protection from harm.*

²⁴ *Some people are so lazy that they won't even lift a finger to feed themselves.*

²⁵ *If you punish a mocker, the simpleminded will learn a lesson; if you reprove the wise, they will be all the wiser.*

²⁶ *Children who mistreat their father or chase away their mother are a public disgrace and an embarrassment.*

²⁷ *If you stop listening to instruction, my child, you have turned your back on knowledge.*

²⁸ *A corrupt witness makes a mockery of justice; the mouth of the wicked gulps down evil.*

²⁹ *Mockers will be punished, and the backs of fools will be beaten.*

Prayer: Lord, I ask that you help me in choosing my friends. I realize that my friends will impact my character. I need your help, because I realize I can be fooled by outward appearances or other surface things. However, I know that you know the heart of a person. Help me to connect with the right people and disconnect from the wrong people. Lord, I thank you for giving me good friends. In Jesus' Name I pray. Amen.

God does not discipline us to subdue us, but to condition us for a life of usefulness and blessedness. (Billy Graham)

Science is organized knowledge,
wisdom is organized life. (Immanuel Kant)

Imagination is more important than knowledge.
(Albert Einstein)

Proverbs 20

Wisdom Instructs on Avoiding Drunkenness, Sloth, and a Contentious Spirit

¹ *Wine produces mockers; liquor leads to brawls. Whoever is led astray by drink cannot be wise.*

² *The king's fury is like a lion's roar; to rouse his anger is to risk your life.*

³ *Avoiding a fight is a mark of honor; only fools insist on quarreling.*

Pearl of Wisdom

350. If your best friends are hurricane and tornado, expect to keep having storms in your life (Prov. 20:3).

⁴ *If you are too lazy to plow in the right season, you will have no food at the harvest.*

⁵ *Though good advice lies deep within a person's heart, the wise will draw it out.*

⁶ *Many will say they are loyal friends, but who can find one who is really faithful?*

⁷ *The godly walk with integrity; blessed are their children after them.*

⁸ *When a king judges, he carefully weighs all the evidence, distinguishing the bad from the good.*

⁹ *Who can say, "I have cleansed my heart; I am pure and free from sin"?*

¹⁰ *The LORD despises double standards of every kind.*

¹¹ *Even children are known by the way they act, whether their conduct is pure and right.*

¹² Ears to hear and eyes to see – both are gifts from the LORD.

¹³ If you love sleep, you will end in poverty. Keep your eyes open, and there will be plenty to eat!

¹⁴ The buyer haggles over the price, saying, "It's worthless," then brags about getting a bargain!

¹⁵ Wise speech is rarer and more valuable than gold and rubies.

¹⁶ Be sure to get collateral from anyone who guarantees the debt of a stranger. Get a deposit if someone guarantees the debt of a foreigner.

¹⁷ Stolen bread tastes sweet, but it turns to gravel in the mouth.

¹⁸ Plans succeed through good counsel; don't go to war without the advice of others.

¹⁹ A gossip tells secrets, so don't hang around with someone who talks too much.

²⁰ If you curse your father or mother, the lamp of your life will be snuffed out.

²¹ An inheritance obtained early in life is not a blessing in the end.

²² Don't say, "I will get even for this wrong." Wait for the LORD to handle the matter.

²³ The LORD despises double standards; he is not pleased by dishonest scales.

²⁴ How can we understand the road we travel? It is the LORD who directs our steps.

²⁵ *It is dangerous to make a rash promise to God before counting the cost.*

²⁶ *A wise king finds the wicked, lays them out like wheat, then runs the crushing wheel over them.*

²⁷ *The LORD's searchlight penetrates the human spirit, exposing every hidden motive.*

²⁸ *Unfailing love and faithfulness protect the king; his throne is made secure through love.*

²⁹ *The glory of the young is their strength; the gray hair of experience is the splendor of the old.*

³⁰ *Physical punishment cleanses away evil; such discipline purifies the heart.*

Pearls of Wisdom

706. The old remind us of the past and the young bring us the future. We need both for balance (Prov. 20:29).

804. Don't expect to find old heads on young shoulders (Prov. 20:29). Wisdom usually comes with time and experience.

Prayer: Lord, I don't need alcohol or any other drug to help me deal with the problems and issues of life. All I need is your power and protection. Help me to have confidence in you and in what you have put in me. I don't need to alter my mind in order to have courage or to make friends. I don't need those things in order to be happy. My joy comes from you and those around me who care about me. I thank you for family and good friends. I praise you for your joy in me in Jesus' Name. Amen.

SECTION V: PROVERBS 21 – 25

Proverbs 21
Wisdom Instructs on Integrity, Patience, and God's Sovereignty

[1] *The king's heart is like a stream of water directed by the LORD; he turns it wherever he pleases.*

[2] *People may think they are doing what is right, but the LORD examines the heart.*

[3] *The LORD is more pleased when we do what is just and right than when we give him sacrifices.*

[4] *Haughty eyes, a proud heart, and evil actions are all sin.*

[5] *Good planning and hard work lead to prosperity, but hasty shortcuts lead to poverty.*

[6] *Wealth created by lying is a vanishing mist and a deadly trap.*

[7] *Because the wicked refuse to do what is just, their violence boomerangs and destroys them.*

[8] *The guilty walk a crooked path; the innocent travel a straight road.*

[9] *It is better to live alone in the corner of an attic than with a contentious wife in a lovely home.*

[10] *Evil people love to harm others; their neighbors get no mercy from them.*

¹¹ *A simpleton can learn only by seeing mockers punished; a wise person learns from instruction.*

¹² *The Righteous One knows what is going on in the homes of the wicked; he will bring the wicked to disaster.*

¹³ *Those who shut their ears to the cries of the poor will be ignored in their own time of need.*

¹⁴ *A secret gift calms anger; a secret bribe pacifies fury.*

¹⁵ *Justice is a joy to the godly, but it causes dismay among evildoers.*

¹⁶ *The person who strays from common sense will end up in the company of the dead.*

¹⁷ *Those who love pleasure become poor; wine and luxury are not the way to riches.*

¹⁸ *Sometimes the wicked are punished to save the godly, and the treacherous for the upright.*

¹⁹ *It is better to live alone in the desert than with a crabby, complaining wife.*

²⁰ *The wise have wealth and luxury, but fools spend whatever they get.*

²¹ *Whoever pursues godliness and unfailing love will find life, godliness, and honor.*

²² *The wise conquer the city of the strong and level the fortress in which they trust.*

²³ *If you keep your mouth shut, you will stay out of trouble.*

²⁴ *Mockers are proud and haughty; they act with boundless arrogance.*

²⁵ *The desires of lazy people will be their ruin, for their hands refuse to work.* ²⁶ *They are always greedy for more, while the godly love to give!*

²⁷ *God loathes the sacrifice of an evil person, especially when it is brought with ulterior motives.*

²⁸ *A false witness will be cut off, but an attentive witness will be allowed to speak.*

²⁹ *The wicked put up a bold front, but the upright proceed with care.*

³⁰ *Human plans, no matter how wise or well advised, cannot stand against the LORD.*

³¹ *The horses are prepared for battle, but the victory belongs to the LORD.*

Prayer: Lord, I praise you for being God all by yourself. I know that you have all the power in heaven and earth in your hands. I know you are everywhere at the same time. I also know that you know everything about me. I know you love me and want what is best for me. I know I can trust you even when I can't trace you. I know you are working on my behalf for your glory and my good. Thank you for being Lord of my life in Jesus' Name. Amen.

Education is the key to liberation because ignorance is the incarceration of the mind. (Rev. Amos L. Lewis)

A mind is a terrible thing to waste.
(The United Negro College Fund)

Proverbs 22

Wisdom Instructs on How to Secure and Keep a Good Name

¹ *Choose a good reputation over great riches, for being held in high esteem is better than having silver or gold.*

² *The rich and the poor have this in common: The LORD made them both.*

³ *A prudent person foresees the danger ahead and takes precautions; the simpleton goes blindly on and suffers the consequences.*

⁴ *True humility and fear of the LORD lead to riches, honor, and long life.*

⁵ *The deceitful walk a thorny, treacherous road; whoever values life will stay away.*

⁶ *Teach your children to choose the right path, and when they are older, they will remain upon it.*

⁷ *Just as the rich rule the poor, so the borrower is servant to the lender.*

Pearls of Wisdom

885. Reputation is who others think you are. Character is who you really are (Prov. 22:1).

553. All behavior is learned -- both good and bad (Prov. 22:6).

714. Character is usually home grown (Prov. 22:6; Eph. 6:1–4).

724. Everything starts at home... good or bad (Prov. 22:6).

976. Children act in public like they act at home (Prov. 22:6).

98. If you aren't debt free, then you're not totally free (Prov. 22:7).

614. Don't spend your future in order to enjoy the present (Prov. 22:7). When you buy what you don't need you steal from yourself.

⁸ *Those who plant seeds of injustice will harvest disaster, and their reign of terror will end.*

⁹ *Blessed are those who are generous, because they feed the poor.*

¹⁰ *Throw out the mocker, and fighting, quarrels, and insults will disappear.*

¹¹ *Anyone who loves a pure heart and gracious speech is the king's friend.*

¹² *The LORD preserves knowledge, but he ruins the plans of the deceitful.*

¹³ *The lazy person is full of excuses, saying, "If I go outside, I might meet a lion in the street and be killed!"*

¹⁴ *The mouth of an immoral woman is a deep pit; those living under the LORD's displeasure will fall into it.*

¹⁵ *A youngster's heart is filled with foolishness, but discipline will drive it away.*

¹⁶ *A person who gets ahead by oppressing the poor or by showering gifts on the rich will end in poverty.*

Thirty Sayings of the Wise

¹⁷ *Listen to the words of the wise; apply your heart to my instruction.* ¹⁸ *For it is good to keep these sayings deep within yourself, always ready on your lips.* ¹⁹ *I am teaching you today – yes, you – so you will trust in the LORD.* ²⁰ *I have written thirty sayings for you, filled with advice and knowledge.* ²¹ *In this way, you may know the truth and bring an accurate report to those who sent you.*

²² *Do not rob the poor because they are poor or exploit the needy in court.* ²³ *For the LORD is their defender. He will injure anyone who injures them.*

24 Keep away from angry, short–tempered people, 25 or you will learn to be like them and endanger your soul.

26 Do not co–sign another person's note or put up a guarantee for someone else's loan. 27 If you can't pay it, even your bed will be snatched from under you.

28 Do not steal your neighbor's property by moving the ancient boundary markers set up by your ancestors.

29 Do you see any truly competent workers? They will serve kings rather than ordinary people.

Prayer: Lord, I realize that there are some things that money cannot buy. In fact, I know the most important things in life are free. I thank you for my reputation. I cherish the good name you have given me in my community of friends. I know if I take care of my character in private you will take care of my reputation in public. Thank you for giving me favor in every area of my life. Help me to maintain my character so that I will always have a good reputation. This is my prayer in Jesus' Name. Amen.

A teacher affects eternity; he can never tell where his influence stops. (Henry Adams)

An educated man should know everything about something, and something about everything.
(C. V. Wedgwood)

Knowledge is the antidote to fear. (Ralph Waldo Emerson)

Proverbs 23

Wisdom Instructs on Greediness, Intemperance, and Impurity

¹ When dining with a ruler, pay attention to what is put before you. ² If you are a big eater, put a knife to your throat, ³ and don't desire all the delicacies – deception may be involved.

Pearls of Wisdom

531. Your outer world is a reflection of your inner world (Prov. 23:7a).

594. Change your focus and you will change your feeling (Prov. 23:7a).

661. Today's thoughts and actions will define your tomorrows (Prov. 23:7a).

786. You are what you think habitually (Prov. 23:7a).

963. We see everything through the tinted glasses of our attitude (Prov. 23:7a).

1107. As a man thinks so is he, and as a man continues to think so will he be (Prov. 23:7a). (Please see the KJV for this verse)

⁴ Don't weary yourself trying to get rich. Why waste your time? ⁵ For riches can disappear as though they had the wings of a bird!

⁶ Don't eat with people who are stingy; don't desire their delicacies. ⁷ "Eat and drink," they say, but they don't mean it. They are always thinking about how much it costs. ⁸ You will vomit up the delicious food they serve, and you will have to take back your words of appreciation for their "kindness."

⁹ Don't waste your breath on fools, for they will despise the wisest advice.

¹⁰ Don't steal the land of defenseless orphans by

moving the ancient boundary markers, ¹¹*for their Redeemer is strong. He himself will bring their charges against you.*

¹²*Commit yourself to instruction; attune your ears to hear words of knowledge.*

¹³*Don't fail to correct your children. They won't die if you spank them.* ¹⁴*Physical discipline may well save them from death.*

¹⁵*My child, how I will rejoice if you become wise.* ¹⁶*Yes, my heart will thrill when you speak what is right and just.*

¹⁷*Don't envy sinners, but always continue to fear the LORD.* ¹⁸*For surely you have a future ahead of you; your hope will not be disappointed.*

¹⁹*My child, listen and be wise. Keep your heart on the right course.* ²⁰*Do not carouse with drunkards and gluttons,* ²¹*for they are on their way to poverty. Too much sleep clothes a person with rags.*

²²*Listen to your father, who gave you life, and don't despise your mother's experience when she is old.* ²³*Get the truth and don't ever sell it; also get wisdom, discipline, and discernment.* ²⁴*The father of godly children has cause for joy. What a pleasure it is to have wise children.* ²⁵*So give your parents joy! May she who gave you birth be happy.*

²⁶*O my son, give me your heart. May your eyes delight in my ways of wisdom.* ²⁷*A prostitute is a deep pit; an adulterous woman is treacherous.* ²⁸*She hides and waits like a robber, looking for another victim who will be unfaithful to his wife.*

²⁹*Who has anguish? Who has sorrow? Who is always fighting? Who is always complaining? Who has unnecessary bruises? Who has bloodshot eyes?* ³⁰*It is the one who*

spends long hours in the taverns, trying out new drinks. [31] *Don't let the sparkle and smooth taste of wine deceive you.* [32] *For in the end it bites like a poisonous serpent; it stings like a viper.* [33] *You will see hallucinations, and you will say crazy things.* [34] *You will stagger like a sailor tossed at sea, clinging to a swaying mast.* [35] *And you will say, "They hit me, but I didn't feel it. I didn't even know it when they beat me up. When will I wake up so I can have another drink?"*

Prayer: Lord, I know I live in a very materialistic world. I am bombarded every day through the internet, email, television, magazines, etc. However, I realize that I don't need a whole lot of expensive things in order to be happy or successful. Help me to be content with what I have. Teach me to be a better manager of the things you have already given me. Lastly, help me to remember that giving is the best cure for greed. Help me to become a generous person. This is my prayer in Jesus' Name. Amen.

Only the educated are free. (Epictetus)

The mind is slow in unlearning what it has been long in learning. (Seneca)

The education of a man is never completed until he dies. (General Robert E. Lee)

What we learn with pleasure we never forget. (Louis Mercier)

Proverbs 24

Wisdom Tells How to Relate to the Wicked and Foolish and Conduct Oneself with Neighbors, and Warns Against Sloth

[1] *Don't envy evil people; don't desire their company.* [2] *For they spend their days plotting violence, and their words are always stirring up trouble.*

Pearl of Wisdom

178. If you want to be successful, always have a good plan and follow it (Prov. 24:3).

[3] *A house is built by wisdom and becomes strong through good sense.* [4] *Through knowledge its rooms are filled with all sorts of precious riches and valuables.*

[5] *A wise man is mightier than a strong man, and a man of knowledge is more powerful than a strong man.* [6] *So don't go to war without wise guidance; victory depends on having many counselors.*

[7] *Wisdom is too much for a fool. When the leaders gather, the fool has nothing to say.*

[8] *A person who plans evil will get a reputation as a troublemaker.* [9] *The schemes of a fool are sinful; everyone despises a mocker.*

[10] *If you fail under pressure, your strength is not very great.*

[11] *Rescue those who are unjustly sentenced to death; don't stand back and let them die.* [12] *Don't try to avoid responsibility by saying you didn't know about it. For God knows all hearts, and he sees you. He keeps watch over*

your soul, and he knows you knew! And he will judge all people according to what they have done.

¹³ My child, eat honey, for it is good, and the honeycomb is sweet to the taste. ¹⁴ In the same way, wisdom is sweet to your soul. If you find it, you will have a bright future, and your hopes will not be cut short.

¹⁵ Do not lie in wait like an outlaw at the home of the godly. And don't raid the house where the godly live. ¹⁶ They may trip seven times, but each time they will rise again. But one calamity is enough to lay the wicked low.

Pearls of Wisdom

730. The best way to keep a secret is to keep it to yourself (Prov. 24:15–16).

687. It's better to do something imperfectly than to do nothing perfectly (Prov. 24:16).

---

¹⁷ Do not rejoice when your enemies fall into trouble. Don't be happy when they stumble. ¹⁸ For the LORD will be displeased with you and will turn his anger away from them.

¹⁹ Do not fret because of evildoers; don't envy the wicked. ²⁰ For the evil have no future; their light will be snuffed out.

²¹ My child, fear the LORD and the king, and don't associate with rebels. ²² For you will go down with them to sudden disaster. Who knows where the punishment from the LORD and the king will end?

More Sayings of the Wise

²³ Here are some further sayings of the wise:

It is wrong to show favoritism when passing judgment. ²⁴ A judge who says to the wicked, "You are innocent," will be cursed by many people and denounced by the nations. ²⁵ *But blessings are showered on those who convict the guilty.*

²⁶ *It is an honor to receive an honest reply.*

²⁷ *Develop your business first before building your house.*

²⁸ *Do not testify spitefully against innocent neighbors; don't lie about them.* ²⁹ *And don't say, "Now I can pay them back for all their meanness to me! I'll get even!"*

³⁰ *I walked by the field of a lazy person, the vineyard of one lacking sense.* ³¹ *I saw that it was overgrown with thorns. It was covered with weeds, and its walls were broken down.* ³² *Then, as I looked and thought about it, I learned this lesson:* ³³ *A little extra sleep, a little more slumber, a little folding of the hands to rest* – ³⁴ *and poverty will pounce on you like a bandit; scarcity will attack you like an armed robber.*

Pearl of Wisdom

652. Those who wait for their ship to come in will realize that its name is hardship (Prov. 24:33–34).

Prayer: Lord, help me not to envy others. I don't want to be someone I'm not. I am happy the way you made me. I celebrate the diversity you have placed in the world. Even though I don't understand some people, I still value them as a human being made in your image. I ask you to make me content with the gifts and talents you have given me. Help me to remember others are there to complete me and not to compete with me. Help me to always value and love people unconditionally in Jesus' Name. Amen.

Proverbs 25

Wisdom Instructs Kings and Their Subjects on the Fear of God and Righteousness

More Proverbs of Solomon

[1] *These are more proverbs of Solomon, collected by the advisers of King Hezekiah of Judah.*

[2] *It is God's privilege to conceal things and the king's privilege to discover them.*

[3] *No one can discover the height of heaven, the depth of the earth, or all that goes on in the king's mind!*

[4] *Remove the dross from silver, and the sterling will be ready for the silversmith.* [5] *Remove the wicked from the king's court, and his reign will be made secure by justice.*

[6] *Don't demand an audience with the king or push for a place among the great.* [7] *It is better to wait for an invitation than to be sent to the end of the line, publicly disgraced! Just because you see something,* [8] *don't be in a hurry to go to court. You might go down before your neighbors in shameful defeat.* [9] *So discuss the matter with them privately. Don't tell anyone else,* [10] *or others may accuse you of gossip. Then you will never regain your good reputation.*

[11] *Timely advice is as lovely as golden apples in a silver basket.*

[12] *Valid criticism is as treasured by the one who heeds it as jewelry made from finest gold.*

[13] *Faithful messengers are as refreshing as snow in the heat of summer. They revive the spirit of their employer.*

¹⁴ *A person who doesn't give a promised gift is like clouds and wind that don't bring rain.*

¹⁵ *Patience can persuade a prince, and soft speech can crush strong opposition.*

¹⁶ *Do you like honey? Don't eat too much of it, or it will make you sick!*

¹⁷ *Don't visit your neighbors too often, or you will wear out your welcome.*

¹⁸ *Telling lies about others is as harmful as hitting them with an ax, wounding them with a sword, or shooting them with a sharp arrow.*

¹⁹ *Putting confidence in an unreliable person is like chewing with a toothache or walking on a broken foot.*

²⁰ *Singing cheerful songs to a person whose heart is heavy is as bad as stealing someone's jacket in cold weather or rubbing salt in a wound.*

²¹ *If your enemies are hungry, give them food to eat. If they are thirsty, give them water to drink.* ²² *You will heap burning coals on their heads, and the LORD will reward you.*

²³ *As surely as a wind from the north brings rain, so a gossiping tongue causes anger!*

²⁴ *It is better to live alone in the corner of an attic than with a contentious wife in a lovely home.*

Pearl of Wisdom

498. Get up and get out or put up with it and shut up (Prov. 25:24; 27:15)! A good relationship or marriage gets better with time while a bad relationship or marriage gets worse with time.

25 Good news from far away is like cold water to the thirsty.

26 If the godly compromise with the wicked, it is like polluting a fountain or muddying a spring.

27 Just as it is not good to eat too much honey, it is not good for people to think about all the honors they deserve.

28 A person without self–control is as defenseless as a city with broken–down walls.

Prayer: Lord, I know that the world is full of bad news. Help me not to watch and read too much negative press so that I am not depressed. I ask that you help me to be a bearer of good news. Help me to share those things that will build people up. Help me to tell people of your love and kindness. I thank you for the good news I've received because of your love, mercy and grace. Now with your help, I will tell others of your love. This is my prayer today in Jesus' Name. Amen.

Education is an ornament in prosperity and a refuge in adversity. (Aristotle)

Everywhere, we learn only from those whom we love. (Johann Wolfgang von Goethe)

What greater work is there than training the mind and forming the habits of the young? (John Chrysostom)

Proverbs 26

Wisdom Instructs against Dishonorable Conduct

¹ *Honor doesn't go with fools any more than snow with summer or rain with harvest.*

² *Like a fluttering sparrow or a darting swallow, an unfair curse will not land on its intended victim.*

³ *Guide a horse with a whip, a donkey with a bridle, and a fool with a rod to his back!*

⁴ *When arguing with fools, don't answer their foolish arguments, or you will become as foolish as they are.*

⁵ *When arguing with fools, be sure to answer their foolish arguments, or they will become wise in their own estimation.*

⁶ *Trusting a fool to convey a message is as foolish as cutting off one's feet or drinking poison!*

⁷ *In the mouth of a fool, a proverb becomes as limp as a paralyzed leg.*

⁸ *Honoring a fool is as foolish as tying a stone to a slingshot.*

⁹ *A proverb in a fool's mouth is as dangerous as a thornbush brandished by a drunkard.*

¹⁰ *An employer who hires a fool or a bystander is like an archer who shoots recklessly.*

¹¹ *As a dog returns to its vomit, so a fool repeats his folly.*

¹² *There is more hope for fools than for people who think they are wise.*

¹³ *The lazy person is full of excuses, saying, "I can't go outside because there might be a lion on the road! Yes, I'm sure there's a lion out there!"*

¹⁴ *As a door turns back and forth on its hinges, so the lazy person turns over in bed.*

¹⁵ *Some people are so lazy that they won't lift a finger to feed themselves.*

¹⁶ *Lazy people consider themselves smarter than seven wise counselors.*

¹⁷ *Yanking a dog's ears is as foolish as interfering in someone else's argument.*

¹⁸ *Just as damaging as a mad man shooting a lethal weapon* ¹⁹ *is someone who lies to a friend and then says, "I was only joking."*

²⁰ *Fire goes out for lack of fuel, and quarrels disappear when gossip stops.*

Pearl of Wisdom

128. Remove bad apples prayerfully and quickly. Low morale is bad for business (Prov. 26:20–28).

---

²¹ *A quarrelsome person starts fights as easily as hot embers light charcoal or fire lights wood.*

²² *What dainty morsels rumors are – but they sink deep into one's heart.*

²³ Smooth words may hide a wicked heart, just as a pretty glaze covers a common clay pot.

²⁴ People with hate in their hearts may sound pleasant enough, but don't believe them. ²⁵ Though they pretend to be kind, their hearts are full of all kinds of evil. ²⁶ While their hatred may be concealed by trickery, it will finally come to light for all to see.

²⁷ If you set a trap for others, you will get caught in it yourself. If you roll a boulder down on others, it will roll back and crush you.

²⁸ A lying tongue hates its victims, and flattery causes ruin.

Prayer: Lord, I pray that you will help me to be a person of honor. Help me not to over commit myself. Help me to prioritize my agenda daily and do the most important things first. If I make a promise, help me to keep it. Help me not to promise what I cannot deliver. Help me to honor all my commitments and make all my appointments. When I cannot make good on my word, help me to be sensitive to others and to call them. Help me to honor you and others at all times. This is my prayer in Jesus' Name. Amen.

I hear and I forget, I see and I remember, I do and I understand. (Chinese Proverb)

Learning is a treasure that will follow its owner everywhere. (Chinese Proverb)

Proverbs 27
Wisdom Instructs on Human Relations

[1] *Don't brag about tomorrow, since you don't know what the day will bring.*

[2] *Don't praise yourself; let others do it!*

[3] *A stone is heavy and sand is weighty, but the resentment caused by a fool is heavier than both.*

[4] *Anger is cruel, and wrath is like a flood, but who can survive the destructiveness of jealousy?*

[5] *An open rebuke is better than hidden love!*

[6] *Wounds from a friend are better than many kisses from an enemy.*

[7] *Honey seems tasteless to a person who is full, but even bitter food tastes sweet to the hungry.*

[8] *A person who strays from home is like a bird that strays from its nest.*

[9] *The heartfelt counsel of a friend is as sweet as perfume and incense.*

[10] *Never abandon a friend – either yours or your father's. Then in your time of need, you won't have to ask your relatives for assistance. It is better to go to a neighbor than to a relative who lives far away.*

[11] *My child, how happy I will be if you turn out to be wise! Then I will be able to answer my critics.*

[12] *A prudent person foresees the danger ahead and takes precautions. The simpleton goes blindly on and suffers the consequences.*

¹³ *Be sure to get collateral from anyone who guarantees the debt of a stranger. Get a deposit if someone guarantees the debt of an adulterous woman.*

¹⁴ *If you shout a pleasant greeting to your neighbor too early in the morning, it will be counted as a curse!*

¹⁵ *A nagging wife is as annoying as the constant dripping on a rainy day.* ¹⁶ *Trying to stop her complaints is like trying to stop the wind or hold something with greased hands.*

¹⁷ *As iron sharpens iron, a friend sharpens a friend.*

¹⁸ *Workers who tend a fig tree are allowed to eat its fruit. In the same way, workers who protect their employer's interests will be rewarded.*

Pearl of Wisdom

188. Without the grinding wheel, the knife remains dull (Prov. 27:17).

---

¹⁹ *As a face is reflected in water, so the heart reflects the person.*

²⁰ *Just as Death and Destruction are never satisfied, so human desire is never satisfied.*

²¹ *Fire tests the purity of silver and gold, but a person is tested by being praised.*

²² *You cannot separate fools from their foolishness, even though you grind them like grain with mortar and pestle.*

²³ *Know the state of your flocks, and put your heart into caring for your herds,* ²⁴ *for riches don't last forever, and the crown might not be secure for the next generation.* ²⁵ *After the hay is harvested, the new crop appears, and the mountain grasses are gathered in,* ²⁶ *your sheep will provide wool for clothing, and your goats will be sold for*

the price of a field. ²⁷ *And you will have enough goats' milk for you, your family, and your servants.*

Prayer: Lord, help me not to brag about what I'm going to do. Help me to acknowledge that you are Lord and that you are in control. Help me to consult you before I make any plans. I want to make sure what I say and do are part of your plan for my life. Help me to also be humble in the success you have given me. I don't want to boast about my accomplishments. I want to give you the glory and praise for making me successful. I want people to see your goodness in my life. Help me to stay humble so that I won't go astray and fall. This is my prayer in Jesus' Name. Amen.

The schools of the country are its future in miniature.
(Tehyi Hsieh)

Just as eating against one's will is injurious to health, so study without a liking for it spoils the memory, and it retains nothing it takes in. (Leonardo Da Vinci)

Good teachers are costly, but bad teachers cost more.
(Bob Talbert)

Give a man a fish and you feed him for a day.
Teach a man to fish and you feed him for a lifetime.
(Chinese Proverb)

Proverbs 28

Wisdom Instructs on the Unscrupulous and Unlawful Dealings of the Rich against the Poor

¹ *The wicked run away when no one is chasing them, but the godly are as bold as lions.*

² *When there is moral rot within a nation, its government topples easily. But with wise and knowledgeable leaders, there is stability.*

³ *A poor person who oppresses the poor is like a pounding rain that destroys the crops.*

Pearls of Wisdom

273. Those who tame lions aren't afraid of dogs (Prov. 28:1).

874. A bold attempt is success (Prov. 28:1; Ps. 27:1-3).

---

⁴ *To reject the law is to praise the wicked; to obey the law is to fight them.*

⁵ *Evil people don't understand justice, but those who follow the LORD understand completely.*

⁶ *It is better to be poor and honest than rich and crooked.*

⁷ *Young people who obey the law are wise; those who seek out worthless companions bring shame to their parents.*

⁸ *A person who makes money by charging interest will lose it. It will end up in the hands of someone who is kind to the poor.*

⁹ *The prayers of a person who ignores the law are despised.*

¹⁰ *Those who lead the upright into sin will fall into their own trap, but the honest will inherit good things.*

¹¹ *Rich people picture themselves as wise, but their real poverty is evident to the poor.*

¹² *When the godly succeed, everyone is glad. When the wicked take charge, people go into hiding.*

¹³ *People who cover over their sins will not prosper. But if they confess and forsake them, they will receive mercy.*

¹⁴ *Blessed are those who have a tender conscience, but the stubborn are headed for serious trouble.*

Pearls of Wisdom

26. When you mess up, admit it and quit it (Prov. 28:13).

378. Repentance is the first step towards restoration and reconciliation (2 Chron. 7:14; Prov. 28:13).

561. When you fail to correct a mistake, you make two mistakes (Prov. 28:13).

¹⁵ *A wicked ruler is as dangerous to the poor as a lion or bear attacking them.*

¹⁶ *Only a stupid prince will oppress his people, but a king will have a long reign if he hates dishonesty and bribes.*

¹⁷ *A murderer's tormented conscience will drive him into the grave. Don't protect him!*

¹⁸ *The honest will be rescued from harm, but those who are crooked will be destroyed.*

¹⁹ *Hard workers have plenty of food; playing around brings poverty.*

²⁰ *The trustworthy will get a rich reward. But the person who wants to get rich quick will only get into trouble.*

²¹ *Showing partiality is never good, yet some will do wrong for something as small as a piece of bread.*

²² *A greedy person tries to get rich quick, but it only leads to poverty.*

²³ *In the end, people appreciate frankness more than flattery.*

²⁴ *Robbing your parents and then saying, "What's wrong with that?" is as serious as committing murder.*

²⁵ *Greed causes fighting; trusting the LORD leads to prosperity.*

²⁶ *Trusting oneself is foolish, but those who walk in wisdom are safe.*

²⁷ *Whoever gives to the poor will lack nothing. But a curse will come upon those who close their eyes to poverty.*

²⁸ *When the wicked take charge, people hide. When the wicked meet disaster, the godly multiply.*

Prayer: Lord, help me to always remember those who are less fortunate than I. I ask you to bless me and make me a blessing. I ask you to touch the hearts of others as well so that they will see the need to help the poor. I ask you to help us empower the poor so at some point they can help themselves. I pray you that you will raise up leaders who will create training programs and jobs to empower the poor. I pray for their health as well as their wealth. I pray that you will make them whole in every area of life. Help all of your children to live in health and prosperity. This I pray in Jesus' Name. Amen.

Proverbs 29

Wisdom Instructs against Stubbornness and Insubordination

¹ *Whoever stubbornly refuses to accept criticism will suddenly be broken beyond repair.*

² *When the godly are in authority, the people rejoice. But when the wicked are in power, they groan.*

³ *The man who loves wisdom brings joy to his father, but if he hangs around with prostitutes, his wealth is wasted.*

⁴ *A just king gives stability to his nation, but one who demands bribes destroys it.*

⁵ *To flatter people is to lay a trap for their feet.*

⁶ *Evil people are trapped by sin, but the righteous escape, shouting for joy.*

⁷ *The godly know the rights of the poor; the wicked don't care to know.*

⁸ *Mockers can get a whole town agitated, but those who are wise will calm anger.*

⁹ *If a wise person takes a fool to court, there will be ranting and ridicule but no satisfaction.*

¹⁰ *The bloodthirsty hate the honest, but the upright seek out the honest.*

¹¹ *A fool gives full vent to anger, but a wise person quietly holds it back.*

¹² *If a ruler honors liars, all his advisers will be wicked.*

¹³ *The poor and the oppressor have this in common – the LORD gives light to the eyes of both.*

[14] *A king who is fair to the poor will have a long reign.*

[15] *To discipline and reprimand a child produces wisdom, but a mother is disgraced by an undisciplined child.*

[16] *When the wicked are in authority, sin increases. But the godly will live to see the tyrant's downfall.*

[17] *Discipline your children, and they will give you happiness and peace of mind.*

[18] *When people do not accept divine guidance, they run wild. But whoever obeys the law is happy.*

[19] *For a servant, mere words are not enough – discipline is needed. For the words may be understood, but they are not heeded.*

[20] *There is more hope for a fool than for someone who speaks without thinking.*

[21] *A servant who is pampered from childhood will later become a rebel.*

Pearls of Wisdom

515. Without a vision the people perish and without people the vision perishes (Prov. 29:18).

563. A dream from God will consume both your mind and time (Gen. 37:5–11; Prov. 29:18).

571. Hot headed people usually have cold hearts (Prov. 29:22).

---

[22] *A hot–tempered person starts fights and gets into all kinds of sin.*

[23] *Pride ends in humiliation, while humility brings honor.*

[24] *If you assist a thief, you are only hurting yourself. You will be punished if you report the crime, but you will be cursed if you don't.*

²⁵ *Fearing people is a dangerous trap, but to trust the LORD means safety.*

²⁶ *Many seek the ruler's favor, but justice comes from the LORD.*

²⁷ *The godly despise the wicked; the wicked despise the godly.*

Prayer: Lord, help me to submit to the authority you have placed over me. Help me to honor my parents. Help me to honor my teachers. Help me to honor my pastor. Help me to honor my boss. Help me to honor government officials as well. I realize you have put these people in authority for my provision, protection and promotion. Help me to stay under the umbrella of your divine order. Help me to honor the chain of command in my life. This is my prayer in Jesus' Name. Amen.

If you don't teach your children the way of the Lord,
the devil will teach them the ways of sin.
(Charles H. Spurgeon)

Education then, beyond all other devices of human origin,
is a great equalizer of the conditions of men, the balance
wheel of the social machinery. (Horace Mann)

Education remains the key to both economic
and political empowerment.
(Congresswoman Barbara Jordan)

Proverbs 30

Wisdom Instructs on God's Word and Other Subjects

The Sayings of Agur

[1] *The message of Agur son of Jakeh. An oracle. I am weary, O God; I am weary and worn out, O God.* [2] *I am too ignorant to be human, and I lack common sense.* [3] *I have not mastered human wisdom, nor do I know the Holy One.*

[4] *Who but God goes up to heaven and comes back down? Who holds the wind in his fists? Who wraps up the oceans in his cloak? Who has created the whole wide world? What is his name – and his son's name? Tell me if you know!*

Pearl of Wisdom

402. Never place your words above God's Word (Prov. 30:5-6).

[5] *Every word of God proves true. He defends all who come to him for protection.* [6] *Do not add to his words, or he may rebuke you, and you will be found a liar.* [7] *O God, I beg two favors from you before I die.* [8] *First, help me never to tell a lie. Second, give me neither poverty nor riches! Give me just enough to satisfy my needs.* [9] *For if I grow rich, I may deny you and say, "Who is the LORD?" And if I am too poor, I may steal and thus insult God's holy name.*

[10] *Never slander a person to his employer. If you do, the person will curse you, and you will pay for it.*

[11] *Some people curse their father and do not thank their mother.* [12] *They feel pure, but they are filthy and unwashed.* [13] *They are proud beyond description and disdainful.* [14] *They devour the poor with teeth as sharp as swords or knives. They destroy the needy from the face of the earth.*

¹⁵ *The leech has two suckers that cry out, "More, more!" There are three other things – no, four! – that are never satisfied:*

¹⁶ *the grave, the barren womb, the thirsty desert, the blazing fire.*

¹⁷ *The eye that mocks a father and despises a mother will be plucked out by ravens of the valley and eaten by vultures.*

¹⁸ *There are three things that amaze me – no, four things I do not understand:*

¹⁹ *how an eagle glides through the sky, how a snake slithers on a rock, how a ship navigates the ocean, how a man loves a woman.*

²⁰ *Equally amazing is how an adulterous woman can satisfy her sexual appetite, shrug her shoulders, and then say, "What's wrong with that?"*

²¹ *There are three things that make the earth tremble – no, four it cannot endure:*

²² *a slave who becomes a king, an overbearing fool who prospers,* ²³ *a bitter woman who finally gets a husband, a servant girl who supplants her mistress.*

²⁴ *There are four things on earth that are small but unusually wise:*

²⁵ *Ants – they aren't strong, but they store up food for the winter.* ²⁶ *Rock badgers – they aren't powerful, but they make their homes among the rocky cliffs.* ²⁷ *Locusts – they have no king, but they march like an army in ranks.* ²⁸ *Lizards – they are easy to catch, but they are found even in kings' palaces.*

29 There are three stately monarchs on the earth – no, four:

30 the lion, king of animals, who won't turn aside for anything, 31 the strutting rooster, the male goat, a king as he leads his army.

32 If you have been a fool by being proud or plotting evil, don't brag about it – cover your mouth with your hand in shame.

33 As the beating of cream yields butter, and a blow to the nose causes bleeding, so anger causes quarrels.

Prayer: Lord, I love your Word. Your Word is my road map in life. I cannot make it successfully through the challenges of life without the wisdom of your Word. Your Word is your Wisdom. I ask that you help me to start and maintain a daily habit of getting into your Word. Your Word will help me live the victorious life. I will cherish your Word by reading it and heeding it. I thank you for your Word. The Bible is the most valuable book I own. Thank for your priceless gift in Jesus' Name I pray. Amen.

It is with books as with men: a very small number play a great part, the rest are lost in the multitude. (Voltaire)

To educate a man in mind and not in morals is to educate a menace to society. (Theodore Roosevelt)

Proverbs 31
Wisdom Instructs Kings and Praises the Virtuous, Wise, and Industrious Woman

The Sayings of King Lemuel

[1] *These are the sayings of King Lemuel, an oracle that his mother taught him.*

[2] *O my son, O son of my womb, O son of my promises,* [3] *do not spend your strength on women, on those who ruin kings.*

[4] *And it is not for kings, O Lemuel, to guzzle wine. Rulers should not crave liquor.* [5] *For if they drink, they may forget their duties and be unable to give justice to those who are oppressed.* [6] *Liquor is for the dying, and wine for those in deep depression.* [7] *Let them drink to forget their poverty and remember their troubles no more.*

[8] *Speak up for those who cannot speak for themselves; ensure justice for those who are perishing.* [9] *Yes, speak up for the poor and helpless, and see that they get justice.*

A Wife of Noble Character

[10] *Who can find a virtuous and capable wife? She is worth more than precious rubies.* [11] *Her husband can trust her, and she will greatly enrich his life.* [12] *She will not hinder him but help him all her life.*

[13] *She finds wool and flax and busily spins it.* [14] *She is like a merchant's ship; she brings her food from afar.* [15] *She gets up before dawn to prepare breakfast for her household and plan the day's work for her servant girls.* [16] *She goes out to*

inspect a field and buys it; with her earnings she plants a vineyard.

[17] *She is energetic and strong, a hard worker.* [18] *She watches for bargains; her lights burn late into the night.* [19] *Her hands are busy spinning thread, her fingers twisting fiber.*

[20] *She extends a helping hand to the poor and opens her arms to the needy.*

[21] *She has no fear of winter for her household because all of them have warm clothes.* [22] *She quilts her own bedspreads. She dresses like royalty in gowns of finest cloth.*

[23] *Her husband is well known, for he sits in the council meeting with the other civic leaders.*

[24] *She makes belted linen garments and sashes to sell to the merchants.*

[25] *She is clothed with strength and dignity, and she laughs with no fear of the future.* [26] *When she speaks, her words are wise, and kindness is the rule when she gives instructions.* [27] *She carefully watches all that goes on in her household and does not have to bear the consequences of laziness.*

[28] *Her children stand and bless her. Her husband praises her:* [29] *"There are many virtuous and capable women in the world, but you surpass them all!"*

Pearl of Wisdom

568. Real beauty is soul deep (Prov. 31:30). Focus on the content rather than the container.

[30] *Charm is deceptive, and beauty does not last; but a woman who fears the LORD will be greatly praised.* [31] *Reward her for all she has done. Let her deeds publicly declare her praise.*

Prayer: Lord, I ask that you give me wisdom in choosing my mate. Once I choose a mate and make a commitment in marriage, help me to honor my commitment by being faithful to my spouse. Help me to be a person of character for my spouse. Help me to focus on inner beauty first. Help me to find a godly partner who loves you. I ask that you will give me a soul mate that will be a blessing to me and not a burden. Thank you for my partner in Jesus' Name. Amen.

Ideas are vehicles that transport us from what is to what could be; leaders are drivers who seek out the best ideas and pilot them into the future. (Justin Pinkerman)

Success is living in such a way that you are using what God has given you — your intellect, abilities, and energy — to reach the purpose that he intends for your life. (Kathi Hudson)

The things which hurt, instruct. (Benjamin Franklin)

A teacher is better than two books. (German Proverb)

The highest result of education is tolerance. (Helen Keller)

Live as if you were to die tomorrow. Learn as if you were to live forever. (Mahatma Gandhi)

IN CLOSING.....

I encourage you to spend at least a whole year going through this book. It takes a while for truth to register. In fact, I've been reading the proverbs off and on for over 30 years. The key to growth is application of the truth.

In fact, Jesus said it a whole lot better than I could ever say it. Notice what he said in Matthew 7:24–27, [24] *"Therefore everyone who hears these words of mine and puts them into practice is like a wise man who built his house on the rock.* [25] *The rain came down, the streams rose, and the winds blew and beat against that house; yet it did not fall, because it had its foundation on the rock.* [26] *But everyone who hears these words of mine and does not put them into practice is like a foolish man who built his house on sand.* [27] *The rain came down, the streams rose, and the winds blew and beat against that house, and it fell with a great crash."* (NIV)

If this book has proven to be a blessing to you, you can find additional resources by visiting the website at:
www.allewisministries.org

I want to thank you from the bottom of my heart for being a part of this ministry by purchasing a copy of this book. I hope these precepts and principles will continue to inspire and guide you as you fulfill your God–given destiny in life. Remember this powerful truth: Wisdom is the master key to all the treasures of life. If you have wisdom, you get everything else you need in life.

If you would like to know God through a personal relationship with Jesus Christ (John 3:16 and John 17:3), then follow the Romans' Road presented on the next page.

Life is short.
Death is sure.
Sin is the problem.
Christ is the cure.
(Author Unknown)

✞

ROMANS' ROAD TO SALVATION

Romans 3:10
As it is written, there is **none righteous**, no not one.

Romans 3:23
For **all have sinned**, and come short of the glory of God.

Romans 6:23
For the **wages of sin is death**; but the gift of God is eternal life through Jesus Christ our Lord.

Romans 5:8
But **God commendeth His love toward us**, in that, while we were yet sinners, Christ died for us.

Romans 10:9-10
That if thou shalt **confess** with thy mouth, the Lord Jesus, and shalt **believe** in thine heart that God hath raised Him from the dead, thou shalt be saved. For with the heart man believes unto righteousness; and with the mouth confession is made unto salvation.

Romans 10:13
For **whosoever shall call** upon the name of the Lord shall be saved. (KJV)

Lord Jesus, I realize that I am a sinner. I believe you died for my sins. Please forgive me of my sins. Come into my heart and be my personal savior. Thank you for saving me and giving me eternal life. In Jesus' Name, I pray, Amen.

> [11] *And this is the testimony: God has given us eternal life, and this life is in his Son.* [12] *He who has the Son has life; he who does not have the Son of God does not have life. (1 John 5:11-12, NIV)*

ABOUT THE AUTHOR

Rev. Amos L. Lewis is the Senior Pastor of the Rising Star Missionary Baptist Church, located in Tucson, Arizona, where he has served for the last 21 years. He is a native of Pinckard, Alabama. After serving in the United States Air Force for 21 years, he decided to make Tucson his home. Rev. Lewis is a gifted teacher and leader. He holds a Masters Degree in Leadership Development. He has taught several classes and workshops at various levels -- local churches, associations, community, and at the state convention. Rev. Lewis shares his ministry with his lovely wife Zeannie Lewis and their four children Kelvin, Jeremiah, Jenelle, and Terria.

CONTACT INFORMATION

If you would like to order more books or if you're interested in other books by Rev. Amos L. Lewis, please visit **www.onechoicecanchangealife.com**, contact A.L.Lewis Ministries at **www.allewisministries.org** or write to Amethyst Moon Publishing, P.O. Box 87885, Tucson, AZ 85754.

CPSIA information can be obtained at www.ICGtesting.com
Printed in the USA
BVOW04s1703041113

335277BV00008B/149/P

9 781935 354062